# EXPLORING KILVERT COUNTRY

Front Cover: View over Clyro towards the Black Mountains

Back Cover: The Old Vicarage at Bredwardine where Francis Kilvert spent the last two years of his life

# EXPLORING KILVERT COUNTRY

Chris Barber

BLORENGE BOOKS

First published 2003

ISBN 1 872730 24 8



All present day photographs are by Chris Barber FRGS

Blorenge Cottage, Church Lane, Llanfoist, Abergavenny,
Monmouthshire NP7 9NG
Tel: 01873 856114

Printed by MWL Print Group Ltd., Units 10/13,
Pontyfelin Industrial Estate, New Inn, Pontypool, Torfaen NP4 ODQ.
Tel: 01495 750033

**ACKNOWLEDGEMENTS**

I am indebted to the many friends and acquaintances who have assisted me in a variety of ways to make the publication of this book possible.

My grateful thanks to:-

Michael Blackmore for providing very fine artwork.

Dr and Mrs Rowe for giving me access to the Kilvert Society archive.

The Kilvert Society for allowing me to make use of the photographic collection.

Barry Smith of the Kilvert Society for checking the walk routes.

Ann Waller for her helpful comments on the manuscript.

Bill Smith of Llowes for the old photograph of Hay Railway Station.

The owners of the Kilvert Gallery for allowing me to see the rooms used by Kilvert when he was in lodgings at Ty Dulas.

Kevin Straw, Rights of Way Maintenance Officer, Powys County Council, for carrying out improvement work on some of the walks.

The numerous residents of Powys, Herefordshire and Monmouthshire, who I encountered on my travels and not only gave help and advice, but also expressed their enthusiasm for my intended publication of this much needed guidebook.

Finally I am most grateful to Adfywio for agreeing to provide financial assistance, thus enabling me to publish the book in colour which is the only way to do full justice to the beautiful scenery in *Kilvert Country*.

*How quiet and sunny and lovely the village was this evening as I went to the Vicarage for dinner. There was not a person in the roads or moving anywhere. The only living creature I saw was a dog. An intense feeling and perception of the extraordinary beauty of the place grew upon me in the silence as I passed through the still sunny churchyard and saw the mountains through the trees rising over the school, and looked back at the church and churchyard through the green arches of the wych elms.*

Rev Francis Kilvert 1871

View over Clyro towards the Black Mountains

# CONTENTS

## Maps

This guidebook is intended to be used with Ordnance Survey maps and while the Landranger series are ideal for the car tours, the best choice for walkers is the Explorer Series.

**Landranger Series** (1:50,000)
147 Elan Valley and Builth Wells
148 Presteigne and Hay-on-Wye
149 Hereford, Leominster
161 Abergavenny and the Black Mountains

**Explorer Series** (1:25,000)
188 Builth Wells
200 Llandrindod Wells & Elan Valley
201 Knighton & Presteigne
13 Brecon Beacons National Park Eastern area

If you intend to lead a party around an unfamiliar walk, particularly one which crosses farmland, it is always advisable to check the route beforehand so that you can be sure of taking your group the correct way and always respect the Country Code. Some of the walks described are quite short strolls, while others are for more energetic walkers wearing suitable footwear. Be prepared for occasional muddy paths, stiles, steep ascents and some map reading.

## The Car Tours

It must be emphasised that most of the routes described involve driving along narrow lanes with few passing places. Reversing will sometimes thus become necessary when meeting oncoming vehicles, so it is a good idea to look out for possible passing places into which you may have to reverse. Hopefully all *Kilvert Country* visitors using this book will be driving in the same direction.

Cyclists may also wish to follow these routes and such a form of transport is the ideal way to explore *Kilvert Country*. Following the intricate web of quiet lanes one can enjoy an intimate appreciation of all the smells, sights and sounds of the beautiful countryside. The many hills to be ascended will also make one very fit!

# PREFACE

The decision to write this guidebook was made during a solitary walk on the remote and mysterious Begwn hills above Clyro in Radnorshire. Visualising the tall bearded Rev Francis Kilvert energetically striding towards Painscastle it suddenly occurred to me that there had not been a guidebook written to the area now known as 'Kilvert Country'. Numerous books about Kilvert himself have been published, but surely there was a need for one which would guide people who came in search of places mentioned in the famous *Diary*.

A few days later, I started work on this new project which was to be my 22nd book. I then spent the best part of three years researching, exploring and photographing all the locations that could be included on the itinerary of any Kilvert enthusiast visiting the area centred on Clyro.

It has been a rewarding and fascinating project and during my many journeys, both by car and on foot, I found the people that I encountered to be most helpful and enthusiastic about the idea of such a guidebook.

Kilvert's happiest times were spent in Clyro where he served as Curate for seven years and this village is undoubtedly the heart of Kilvert Country. But the area as a whole is complex and difficult to get to know, particularly for anyone making a brief visit. Thus my purpose has been to compile an easy to follow, but comprehensive introduction to the area associated with the Reverend Francis Kilvert.

Following in Kilvert's footsteps I visited the secret little valleys, hamlets and little churches in the rolling hills above Clyro, which otherwise I may never have seen. During my wanderings I was also intrigued to find that so many stories concerning the roaming curate are preserved in the folklore of this area. Such enduring memories are due to the fact that this sensitive man was regarded with great respect and affection by parishioners, both rich and poor. His social graces took him into the grand homes of the gentry and the humblest of cottages. By holding up a mirror to the past he provided us with cameos of country life in mid Victorian times. Yet on my travels, I came to realise that the unspoilt countryside of Radnorshire that he once knew so well has changed very little. Yes, many of the lanes that he followed have been changed from rough tracks to tarmac roads and some of the mills, cottages and farms that he visited are now ruined, but the solitude and beauty of the landscape is still very special.

Although not writing for intended publication, Kilvert wrote for posterity, or at least in the hope that someone in the future might read what he had written. Selections from his Diary were published in 1938 are still read with pleasure by people all over the world and the Kilvert Society formed in 1947 has more than six hundred members.

My work now completed, I invite you to follow in my own footsteps to explore the world described by Francis Kilvert. The journeys described in this book will take you to remote little churches, guide you to the lonely cwm where 'the Solitary' of Llanbedr once resided, and the well concealed cave where Prince Llywellyn spent his last night. I suggest you climb the steep mound of Snodhill Castle, where Kilvert and his friends once enjoyed a sumptuous picnic. At the quaint little church of Colva make sure you try out the echo, described by Kilvert as 'plain and clear', then descend to Newchurch to visit the grave of little Emmeline.

From Clyro you can follow the route frequently taken by Kilvert across the green fields to Hay-on-Wye, with the brooding Black Mountains ever present in the distance. From this now famous book town, ascend into these mountains and cross the lonely Gospel Pass to reach the little whitewashed church at Capel-y-ffin, which Kilvert tells us, 'reminded him of an owl'. Then follow the narrow lane through the Vale of Ewyas to Llanthony and explore the ruined Priory before enjoying the hospitality of the Abbey Hotel just like Kilvert did in 1870.

On another day, follow the beautiful Wye Valley, via Glasbury, Erwood, Aberedw, Builth Wells, Newbridge and Rhayader. Then continue north to the little village of St Harmons where Kilvert was Vicar for just one year.

Finally, travel east into Herefordshire to reach Monnington-on-Wye, where Kilvert's description is still true today: 'so calm and so serene - no hurry, no crowds, no confusion, no noise.'

Your journey will end in the delightful village of Bredwardine where Kilvert became Vicar in 1877 and lived in an attractive whitewashed house overlooking a beautiful stretch of the River Wye. It was here that he spent his final days, and wrote the last pages of his *Diary*. A simple cross marks his grave and also the end of this magical journey through the lovely countryside of Radnorshire, Monmouthshire and Herefordshire.

I hope that you enjoy *Exploring Kilvert Country* just as much as I did and that this book is of assistance to you on your travels.

Chris Barber<br>Llanfoist<br>May 2003

# INTRODUCTION

Francis Kilvert was born in December 1840 at Hardenhuish, near Chippennham, Wiltshire and his father was rector of that parish. As a youngster Francis was probably educated privately, first at his father's school in the rectory, and then by his uncle (also named Francis) who ran a private school in Bath. In 1859 he went to Oxford where he studied for the priesthood at Wadham College, taking his B.A. in 1862 and his M.A. in 1866.

By then he was serving as a curate to his father, who had become Rector at Langley Burrell, Wiltshire. In November 1864 he was interviewed at Clyro in Radnorshire for the position of curate. The Vicar, Richard Lister Venables wrote to his brother, George Steven Venables:

> *'I have got a young fellow here named Kilvert about the curacy and I believe it is settled. He seems to be a gentleman and I like what I have seen. He is quite young and will not be in Priest's Orders till Christmas. The Bishop of Gloucester and Bristol has agreed to his leaving his present curacy, which is his father's, and after the ordination, and from the tone of the Bishop's letter which he sent me it is evident that he is respectable. However he has referred me to a Cannon Shirley at Christchurch, and I have written to him as a matter of precaution. He is tall with a black beard and moustache. It will be a great satisfaction to have got this matter hopefully settled.'*

A month later, Kilvert was ordained Priest in Bristol Cathedral and he arrived in Clyro in January 1865, taking lodgings with Mrs Chaloner at Ty Dulas (now called Ashbrook House). His decision to leave Langley Burrell for remote Clyro must have seemed very strange to his family and friends, but for this young curate, his time in Radnorshire was to prove a period of considerable happiness and fulfilment. In total he spent seven years as curate at Clyro and then in 1872 returned to Langley Burrell. Four years later he took up the living of St Harmon's in Radnorshire, but was only there for just under twelve months. He reached the pinnacle of his career in 1877 when he became Vicar of Bredwardine, Herefordshire and married two years later. But sadly, just five weeks after his wedding, he died of peritonitis on 23rd September 1879.

The brief story of this young Victorian clergyman would have passed into oblivion had he not in 1870 begun writing a diary which has provided us with a fascinating record of the last nine years of his life. During each day, he made notes in a small pocket book which were transferred to the main *Diary* later, sometimes before breakfast on the following morning.

What is surprising is the fact that Kilvert had first arrived in Clyro in 1865, but it was not until January 1870 that the *Diary* commences and it has been suggested that it was the result of a New Year's Resolution. However it is possible that the first five years of his record have not been found. It is unfortunate that the details of these years are not available, but with occasional gaps the *Diary* runs from January 1870 to March 1877 and originally consisted of some thirty notebooks containing well over a million words.

The *Diary* was written up almost every day, providing a chatty commentary on what Kilvert had seen or heard and how the country folk who lived around him were spending their lives. He faithfully put down everything that came to his attention, providing an intimate account of country life in the Welsh Border and also Wiltshire, which he visited occasionally. Not only did he write about his encounters with people, but he also vividly described scenery, weather, and the surrounding countryside.

Kilvert was a keen and accurate observer of birds and wild flowers and took particular delight in the woods, streams and dingles through which he passed on his frequent long solitary walks. His descriptions show that he was particularly sensitive to storms, dazzling white clouds and bursts of sunlight.

He comes over as a very kind and sociable man who had a great affection for children and he abhorred violence. In the course of his parochial duties he saw much poverty and we are given glimpses of how difficult life was for country folk of very limited means in the mid-Victorian age. For example he tells of visiting a squalid cottage where he finds a dying man of eighty-two and a fair-haired girl of four having to share the same bedroom.

By contrast Kilvert was also a regular visitor to many of the grand mansions in the area where he was welcomed by the wealthy gentry who took him into their hearts. His social circle included numerous reasonably affluent families: the Baskervilles of Clyro Court, the Morrells of Cae Mawr, the Crichtons of Wyecliff, the Venables at Clyro Vicarage, the Allens of Clifford Priory the Thomas's of Llanthomas, the Hamers of Boatside, the Dews of Whitney and the Bevans of Hay Castle. He joined these 'well to do' folk in their games of croquet on the lawn, enjoyed the tea and strawberries that followed and participated with ease in the cultured conversations.

His *Diary* reveals that he had a weakness for beautiful women and a particular fondness for little girls. He tells us how he would walk, 'ten miles for a kiss', and how in 1870 he became infatuated with ten-year old Elizabeth Jones, whom he called Gipsy Lizzie.

The only known photograph of the Rev Francis Kilvert, taken when he was about 30 years of age

Then there was Miss Lyne who had *a beautiful little hand, just what a lady's hand ought to be, small, soft, white, warm and dry.*

In today's society Kilvert's fascination for little girls would have been viewed with considerable alarm and he would have probably got into serious trouble with the authorities. However, in his case, such behaviour was no doubt little more than the innocent affection of a very sincere young man who wished one day to be happily married with children of his own.

The great love of his life was 'Daisy' Thomas of Llanthomas in the parish of Llanigon and Kilvert confides in his *Diary*: *Today I fell in love with Fanny Thomas.* He was heartbroken when her father refused to allow him to become engaged to her.

Kilvert not only describes locations in Radnorshire, Herefordshire and Wiltshire, but he also travelled widely visiting such places as North Wales, Somerset, Dorset, Devon, Cornwall, the Isle of Wight, London, Oxford, Bath, Bristol and elsewhere.

While living at Clyro Kilvert was often catching trains at Hay and changing trains at Three Cocks. Also, he would often get out at Whitney Station to visit Whitney vicarage or Whitney Court. Some years later, while vicar of Bredwardine, he would walk to Kinnersley or Moorhampton and catch a train to Hay or Hereford. There were eight daily passenger trains between Hereford and Brecon - four each way - with no trains on Sundays.

Sometimes he walked from Clyro across the hills to Aberedw station, where trains stopped on a signalled request, and he then returned home via Three Cocks and Hay. The present-day station at Builth Road was already a junction with the line from Swansea to Shrewsbury, while the Mid-Wales station, which was established first, was called Llechryd.

This energetic young man was a tireless walker who sometimes covered twenty-five miles in a day but not having the benefit of detailed maps showing footpaths he had to rely on local knowledge and signposts. When in doubt he would often ask someone who would always politely point him in the right direction. But there were obviously times when he lost his way, particularly during his early rambles from Clyro and the following extract serves as a good example of such route finding problems:

> *From Wye Cliff I went on through ceaseless rain by the Wye-side meadow path to Llowes, passing by the Old Barn. As I crossed these meadows I saw a cuckoo flying from tree to tree for the first time this spring. Above Pwlldwrgi the nine great poplar spies shone with a golden light even through the rain, and all the spouts and springs and pistylls along the Brunant and Llowes banks were roaring wild and strong...*

*I passed through the village and went up by Ciluni Dingle sides in search of the Upper Noyadd. Up and up I went past Moity and the chapel, the road growing narrower, steeper and stonier, till at length from a lane it threatened to become a watercourse and the rain growing harder till I seemed to be amongst the clouds. I began to suspect that I had lost the way, and seeing a farmhouse a little distance to the left of the lane amongst some fields I turned my steps thither to inquire the way. The farmhouse was full of dogs and children. A rosy-faced girl came to the door, and in answer to my questions told me the name of the place but I could not quite catch it. I think it was the Gaer. She turned back to someone in the kitchen behind her saying, 'Here's a man wants to know the way to Clyro.' At this moment three men came from the fold round the corner of the farmhouse. One of them was tall, black-haired, broad-shouldered and long-legged, a true Radnorshire man. I repeated my question to him.*

*'There's a little village called Llowes down below,' said he in a high squealing voice. 'Go you down to him.' 'But,' I explained, 'I have just come up from Llowes. I don't want to go down there again. I want to go across the hills to Clyro. Which is the way please?' 'There is no way,' said the man confidently. 'You will never find it. There is a great dingle between. I have lived here fifteen years and I have never been able to find the way.' And he was turning into the house in a huff, when I stopped him once more and asked him to tell me the way to Upper Noyadd. 'Yes, you can go to Upper Noyadd,' he said. 'Go you down to Moity by the chapel and there they will tell you the way.' I thanked him and was turning away in the pouring rain when the black-haired tall man said sharply and quickly, 'Make so bold, what's your name?' I told him. 'Gilvert,' he said rolling the name round in his mouth as if it were a hot potato. 'Gilvert. Are you a minister?' 'Yes,' I said. 'Are you a preacher?' 'Yes,' I said, though I added to myself, not the kind of preacher you mean. 'Then,' said he heartily,'come you in and take something to drink.' I assured him with thanks that I was much too wet already and went my way. The mountain farmer thought evidently that I was a wandering Dissenting minister.*

It is surprising that he did not appear to use a map for the first edition of the Ordnance Survey map had been on sale for about forty years. The absence of a map would certainly explain Kilvert's mainly phonetic spelling of place names and the fact that his versions were very different to those of Ordnance Survey. He had no doubt never seen many of these names written down and he spelt them just as he heard them spoken by the local people.

As far as we know Kilvert only showed his *Diary* to just one friend but it does seem possible that even though it was primarily kept for his own personal satisfaction, he also had a vague hope that someone in the future might read what he had written, for he once commented:

> *Why do I keep this voluminous journal? I can hardly tell. Partly because life appears to me such a curious and wonderful thing that it almost seems a pity that even such a humble and uneventful life as mine should pass away without some record as this, and partly too because I think the record may amuse and interest some who come after me.*

After Kilvert's death most of his notebooks were preserved by his family and in 1938 twenty-two of them were placed by his nephew T. Perceval Smith in the hands of William Plomer, of the London publishing firm Jonathan Cape with a view to their publication. Plomer was intrigued by the *Diary* which he later described as *'written in a sloping hand, and proved so interesting that it was decided to prepare it for publication. There was too much material to print all at once, and it was not all of equal interest. I proceeded therefore to take the cream of the first 8 notebooks, and the resulting volume contains roughly one-third of their contents.*

*There is little to be said about my method of selection except that I have tried to be as careful as possible to eliminate everything of merely fugitive interest and to retain everything that seemed most worth preserving and offering to the reading public.'*

Between 1938 and 1940, William Plomer published three volumes of the Diary which were well received by a wide readership and *Kilvert's Diary* was quickly established as one of the minor classics of English Literature. In due course it was to be read by a world-wide audience.

The published material fills about 1,200 pages but in fact only represents about one-third of the original manuscript. In 1948 William Plomer commented, *'Kilvert enthusiasts have sometimes said to me, "Why can't we have the whole thing?" I don't believe they would necessarily be pleased to have it, and to print it would be an enormous and perhaps unjustifiable and a very costly undertaking. I think I can assure you that the best and most essential parts of the Diary are in print. I left out what seemed to me commonplace and trivial, so you only know Kilvert at his most vivid.'*

Mrs Essex Hope was the last person to own the 22 notebooks in which Kilvert's Diary was compiled. Unfortunately, she decided that the contents were much too personal and with the exception of three, destroyed them.

Dr William Plomer addressing members of the Kilvert Society

Following the death of T. Perceval Smith the twenty-two notebooks were inherited by his sister, Mrs Essex Hope, who unfortunately decided that the contents of the Diaries were too personal and apart from three, burnt them. She gave away these three surviving notebooks to: Charles Harvey of Birmingham (now held by the National Library of Wales), the playwright Jeremy Sandford (later deposited at Durham University) while the third one was given to William Plomer. It has been estimated that if all the notebooks were available there would be sufficient material to fill nine volumes instead of just three. Tragically, all copies of William Plomer's transcripts of the notebooks were accidentaly destroyed.

There were gaps in the *Diary* between September 1875 and March 1876 and between June 1876 and December 1877 while the last entry is on Thursday, 13th March, 1879, just a few months before Kilvert's death. It is of course possible that there was a subsequent notebook which has not been discovered or has not survived. In his last entry Kilvert is still on his country visits and admiring the Wye Valley as he goes. For example, he speaks of a lovely cloudless day, and views of the Black Mountains with their snow patches. He walks home to Bredwardine from Kinnersley and concludes, *A sharp frost and the north-west wind bitterly cold.*

Anyone who reads Kilvert's *Diary* cannot fail to appreciate the literary skill with which he describes so many fascinating aspects of a way of life that has long since vanished. Francis Kilvert comes over as a man with a sense of humour, a genuine interest in people and with a great zest for life. His journal is undoubtedly a social document of unique importance which provides the finest record of provincial parochial life in the 1870's that has ever been compiled.

## OLD RADNORSHIRE

The old county of Radnorshire covers an area of 470 square miles and it contains some of the most beautiful scenery in Wales, which caused the poet Shelley to comment: *'Nature is here marked with the most impressive characteristics of loveliness and grandeur.'*

Also impressed with Radnorshire was the playwright, George Bernard Shaw who once remarked that *'no man ought to be in the government of this land, who did not spend three months of every year in such a countryside.'*

In shape the county of Radnorshire bears a close resemblance to Africa, and is about 26 miles from north to south, while from east to west it measures 29 miles. More than half of this area is above the 1,000 foot contour and there are no less than one hundred hills rising to more than 1,500 feet above sea level.

Not surprisingly, it is one of the most sparsely populated regions south of the Scottish border, with barely twenty people to the square mile. In fact one is likely to encounter more sheep than people. This statement is certainly confirmed by an Agricultural Census taken in 1971 which gives the numbers of sheep and lambs in the county as 652,971. The population figure given at that time was just less than 20,000 which represented 139 persons per square mile.

It is an ancient land rich in antiquities. There are the remains of at least eight prehistoric stone circles, as well as numerous standing stones and burial mounds of the Bronze Age going back 3,000 years or more. Hardly a town or village in Radnorshire is without a castle site, although little remains today of the stone fortresses except their foundations. They were mainly built by the Norman Lords Marchers, who ruled this Borderland having been allowed by the monarch to keep as much Welsh territory as they could conquer. Through the centuries their castles were taken and re-taken. Ultimately, they were either destroyed or collapsed and stone by stone were carted away for other purposes. Many of them stood in forlorn and lonely places and although their history is now vague and incomplete their mounds are long enduring.

The high ground is open moorland, where cart-tracks merge into footpaths and the solitude is only broken by the cry of the buzzard or the call of the curlew and other birds. Wild ponies roam freely and the multitude of Radnor sheep, which are a different breed from the Welsh mountain sheep of other counties are world famous. The Radnor sheep is short-limbed and low set, with speckled face and legs and is related to the Clun Forest and Kerry Hill variety.

# The Old County of Radnorshire

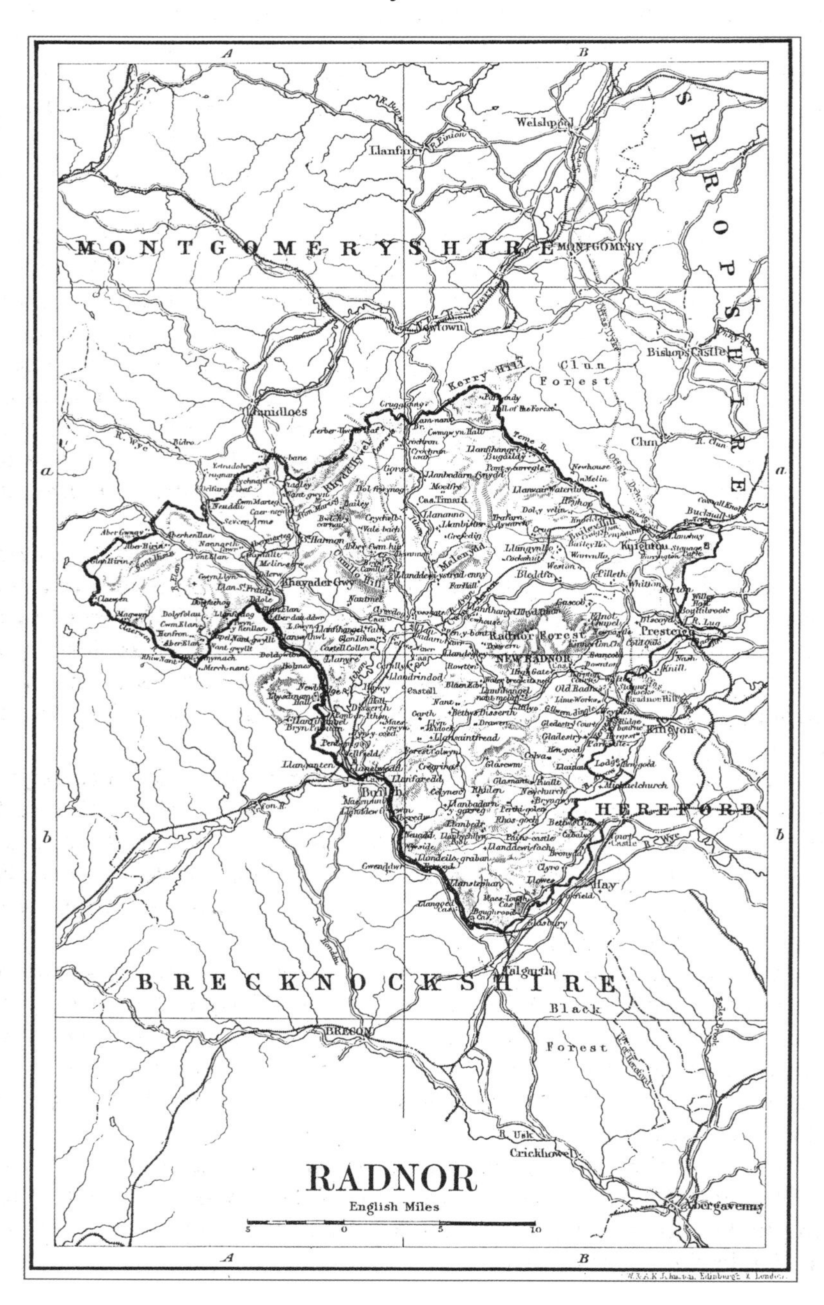

The medieval name for the area was Rhwng Gwy a Hafren, meaning the land 'between the Wye and the Severn'. But during the reign of Henry VIII the area was finally delivered from the Lords Marchers and in 1536 it became the County of Radnorshire under English law. It would seem that during the next century the county Squires did not forget this, and loyally took the King's side in the Civil War. Charles I was no doubt grateful for such support for he twice found welcome refuge in Radnorshire farmhouses when in retreat from Parliamentary forces.

The old churches of Radnorshire are usually long low buildings with a squat massive tower, built for defence rather than ornament. Seldom are they to be found in a village, but usually mark the centre of a scattered district, standing in solitary isolation on a hillock among ancient yew trees and accessed by a grass track leading from the nearest road. They are some of the most beautiful churches in Wales, generally small, but often filled with remarkable rich woodwork and sculpture. There are fifty or more churches in the county and thirty-one have been rebuilt, and while few have escaped the misguided work of the Victorian 'restorers' no less than seventeen screens have survived.

A number of these churches stand in circular graveyards, indicating very early foundation and indeed several of them stand on prehistoric burial grounds thus linking the old and new religions. St Harmon's Church is a good example for it stands on a mound within a circular churchyard. Founded by St Harmon (Garmon) in the fifth century, it is said that in the first simple church on this site the Saint and his clergy prayed against the sins of the tyrant Vortigern.

Radnorshire has long been noted as a county rich in folklore, legends and superstitions which all proved of great interest to Kilvert. During his parochial visits he came across many old folk who were unable to read or write, but could talk at length of local superstitions and traditional tales. These had never been written down but just passed on orally from generation to generation.

Superstition undoubtedly played an important part in Clyro life, especially among the older folk, who for example would be most worried if the first black snail of the year was met crawling on the hard road, instead of on grass - for this would mean a bad season. To destroy a swallow's nest was most unlucky and parsley must never be transplanted but always sown.

A pewter plate was always placed on the coffin lid the night before a burial, and a lighted candle set upon the plate. It was also not the done thing to be buried on the north side (or 'back-side') of the church for that was the devil's special domain.

It was considered very unlucky to hide iron before one died, for the spirit could not rest and would always come back to look for it. An old woman told Kilvert how a penknife had once been hidden in a yew tree near Llanships Farm, and after the funeral there was no rest day or night. The spirit kept rumbling and rummaging about the place, hunting for this hidden iron. Then late at night earthenware plates began to fall with loud crashes off the kitchen shelves, but were found to be unbroken on the floor. They were replaced and the same thing happened time and time again, yet remarkably the plates were never broken.

This same old woman Kilvert tells us, had a curious way of finding out the thief when anything had been stolen. She would put the key of the house door into the Bible, on the verse, *'Where thou goest I will go', and then, would name the persons she suspected, saying at the same time, 'Said St Peter to St Paul, turn you or turn you not?' At the name of the thief, so she claimed, the key would turn*.

Kilvert described how birch and withan (rowan) were hung on the cottage doors against the charm of witches, but added, *but the young witches are welcome*. He quotes many examples of old beliefs in Radnorshire. For example when boys returning home from market would turn their caps back to front, so that they would not be enticed into fairy rings to dance. It was believed that fairies lingered in Radnorshire long after they had disappeared from the rest of Wales and were last seen at Llanbwchllyn Pool, below the precipitous rocks of Penycwm, near Llanbedr Church.

On December 8, 1870, Kilvert recorded in his *Diary* that he had been talking about fairies with Dave Price who lived near Capel-y-ffin. Price told him:

> *We don't see them now because we have more faith in the Lord Jesus and don't think of them. But I believe the fairies travel yet. My sister's son, who works at the collieries in Monmouthshire, once told me he saw the fairies dancing to beautiful music, sweet music, in a Monmouthshire field. They all came over a stile close by him. They were very yellow in the face, between yellow and red, and dressed almost all in red. He did not like to see them. He fully believes in them and so do I.*

Kilvert also talked with Old Hannah Whitney on this subject. In 1870 at the age of ninety, she told him how as a child of eight or nine she used to listen to her grandfather and his friends telling tales about the fairies, in which they fully believed.

Radnorshire girls used to sow hemp-seed on All Hallowmas Eve to see their future phantom lovers mowing the crop the same night and at one Radnor parish, the people used to go to the church door at midnight *to hear the saints within call the names of those to die that year*.

People in Clyro, on Twelfth Night, used to go out to watch the cattle kneel and one farmer assured Kilvert that he had indeed seen his own cattle kneel as the cock crowed. He maintained that only seven-year old cattle went on their knees and the young beasts were never known to do so.

An interesting event which Kilvert observed on Twelfth night was the famous custom of Mari Lwyd - 'Blessed Mary' - which seemed to him to be the relic of an old Miracle Play:

> *It was between the Christmases, and at eight o' clock I was sitting with some other people around the fire, when we heard tramping outside, and a loud knocking on the door, which was locked. There was the sound of a flute a moment later, and a man was singing - I could not distinguish the words - then a few minutes later another man, inside the room, went to the door and sang what was apparently an answer to the song without. Then the door was thrown open, and in walked about a dozen people, headed by a most extraordinary apparition, an animal covered with a flowing sheet, and surmounted by a horse's skull, to which a bridle was attached. This apparition, I saw a moment later was really a man covered with a sheet; his head was bowed down, and a skull had been fastened on to it. The people sang, collected some money, and then went off. They ought by rights, apparently to have had an ass's skull, but then dead donkeys, are proverbially hard to come by!*

To the north of Clyro is an area of secret little valleys, little churches, remote chapels, wooded dingles, rippling streams and rolling hills. For the Rev. Francis Kilvert it was an earthly paradise and so much of this countryside is still remarkably unchanged since his wanderings in the 1870s. One can follow a maze of steep-banked lanes decorated with primroses, fragrant wild violets and delicious wild strawberries, topped by hedges of honeysuckle and dog-rose.

One does not hear Welsh spoken in Radnorshire for the extinction of the language was hastened by the custom of appointing monoglot English clergy to the Welsh-speaking parishes. This occurred in spite of endless petitions from the parishioners for Welsh-speaking bishops and clergy.

A typical scene in the beautiful county of Old Radnorshire

St Harmons was the last parish church in the county to have services which were conducted entirely in Welsh until about 1835, and afterwards one Welsh service a month was held until 1865. But the Nonconformists carried on having Welsh services much longer than the churches. Kilvert recorded that the last Welsh speaking native died in 1867.

Although the Welsh language is now completely absent in Radnorshire, the Welsh intonation and influence has remained in many of the words and phrases still in use and in the local pronounciations of the Welsh place names, even when much corrupted by English spelling. Radnorshire folk always seem ready to talk and one leaves with the feeling that it is a very hospitable area as indeed the Rev Francis Kilvert certainly found during his seven years as Curate of Clyro.

*'Despite its loss of the Welsh language, let us hope that Radnorshire will ever keep its Welsh names in remembrance, as part of its ancient heritage. Wild Wales dwells in every corner of its hills and sheep-banked villages. Welsh it is by birth and tradition. Welsh may it always remain, in spirit if not in the spoken word.'*

W.H. Howse *Radnorshire* 1949

# WALK 1

## *Kilvert's Clyro*

1 ¾ miles (3km)

*I looked down upon the dear old village nestling round the Church in the hollow at the dingle mouth and saw the fringes of the beautiful woods and the hanging orchards and the green slopes of Penllan and the white farms and cottages dotted over the hills a thousand sweet and sad memories came over me and all my heart rose up within me and went out in love towards the beloved place and people among whom I lived so long and so happily.*

Rev Francis Kilvert

Clyro (pronounced Cligh-roe) was previously known as Cleirwy and in the eleventh century this ancient settlement was a possession of Einion Clyd, Lord of Elfael. The village is situated just inside Radnorshire and within a mile of the meeting point of old Breconshire and Herefordshire. It once straddled the busy Hereford to Brecon road (A483) but was fortunately by-passed on its east side in the 1960s. By contrast the road running through the centre of the village was just a quiet lane in Kilvert's time.

St Michael's Church, Clyro, where Kilvert was curate for seven years (1865 -1872)

A famous incident in the history of Clyro concerns Trehearn Vaughan, a local nobleman, who incurred the wrath of William de Braose, Lord of Abergavenny. With his usual cunning, de Braose invited Trehearn to a friendly get-together but then attacked him. The poor man was tied to a horse's tail, dragged through Brecon, then beheaded and his body hung from a gallows.

Gwenwynwyn, Prince of Powys, a relative of Vaughan, swore that he would avenge his death by sweeping de Braose's land as clean as the palm of his hand and he made plans to attack William's fortress at Painscastle in the hills to the north of Clyro. But de Braose was well prepared to do battle, having summoned all his friends and vassals and also Gwenwynwyn's rivals. A terrible battle was fought near Painscastle in which three thousand Welshmen were killed and Gwenwynwyn was defeated.

When Kilvert arrived in Clyro in 1865, the village had a population of about 850 and there were two inns, two smiths, a saddler, a shoemaker, a tailor, two millers, two carpenters and a threshing machine driver. It is from his *Diary* that we are able to gain a detailed picture of the village and its inhabitants at that time.

> *Old Hannah Whitney was sitting in her cottage door at work as usual with her high cap and her little red shawl pinned over her breast, her thin grey-bearded nutcracker face bent earnestly upon her knitting till she glanced sharply up over her spectacles to see who it was that was passing.*

**St Michael's Church** with its rectangular crenellated tower, capped by a gilded weather-cock, is a typical reconstructed Victorian village church. The plinth of the tower is the only remaining part of the 12th century building for it was rebuilt in 1852. But the circular churchyard serves to remind us that it stands on an ancient site. Rebuilding took place in 1853 and its somewhat austere interior has probably changed very little since Kilvert's time.

Contained in the embattled tower are five bells which were recast and rehung in 1887. The tower was restored and raised in 1894 at the expense of Walter T. Mynors Baskerville of Clyro Court and two years later he also paid for a clock to be placed on the outside of the tower.

Inside the church a St Cecilia window commemorates Cecilia Macfarlane of Clyro Vicarage (1872-1899), 'who led the singing in the choir here for many years.' The East window was erected by the wife and children of Thomas Mynors Baskerville in his memory.

Francis Kilvert's sister, Dora, made this sketch of Clyro Church, with its low western tower, with saddleback roof in the spring of 1865. By the end of that year the tower was heightened and given a battlemented top. We can see that previously, it was a modest building similar to those that have remained unchanged, in the hills north of Clyro, such as Bryngwyn and Llandewi Fach.

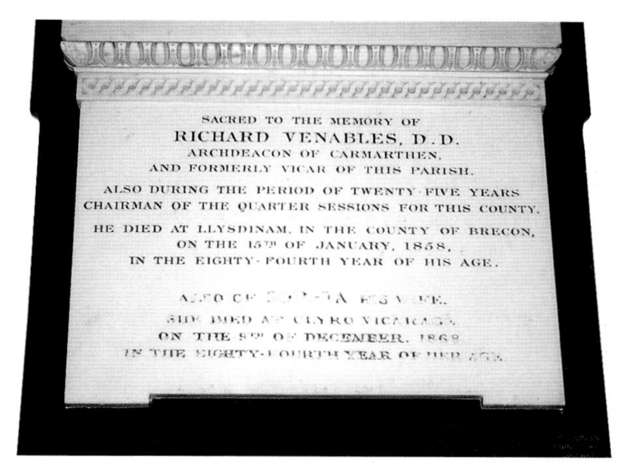


Plaque in Clyro Church commemorating Richard Venables, Archdeacon of Carmarthen and formerly Vicar of Clyro, who died at Llysdinam in 1868 at the age of 84.

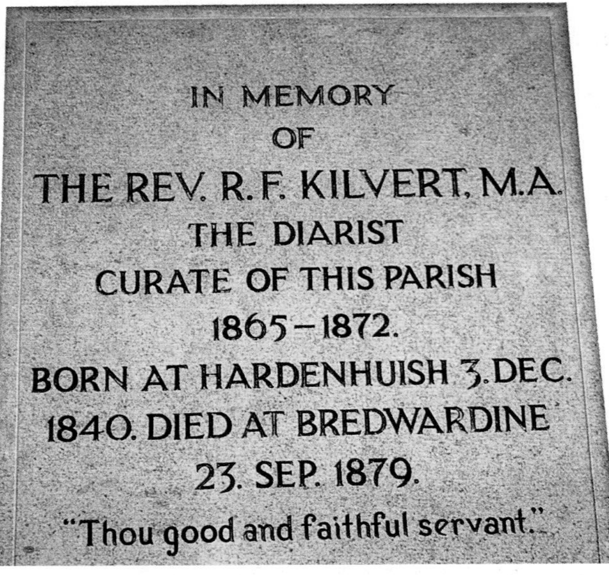

This plaque commemorating the life of the Rev Francis Kilvert was unveiled in 1949 (the first year of the Kilvert Society) by Robert Wyn Kilvert, the great-nephew of the Diarist.

Francis Kilvert spent seven years as Curate at Clyro (1856-72) and is commemorated with a wall tablet. On the same wall there is a framed photograph showing him with his bushy black beard, seated and holding a book.

The large churchyard crowded with headstones reminds one of the time that Kilvert walked through it, the day after Christmas Eve and recorded in his Diary how the flowered graves looked like people asleep in the moonlight, *ready to rise early on Easter Morning*.

When Kilvert arrived in Clyro the population was about 850. It reached a peak of 1,000 in later years and then fell considerably. In the 1960s Clyro was by-passed by the A483 and the loss of through traffic resulted in a degree of peace returning to the village.

*The beauty of the view, the first view of the village, coming down by the Brooms this evening was indescribable. The brilliant golden poplar spires shone in the evening light like flames against the dark hill side of the Old Forest and the blossoming fruit trees, the torch trees of Paradise blazed with a transparent green and white lustre up the dingle in the setting sunlight. The village is in a blaze of fruit blossom. Clyro at its loveliest. What more can be said?*

Plaque commemorating Ralph Hopton Baskerville of Clyro Court, who was killed in action during the First World War at the age of 35. He was the son of Kilvert's Squire and heir to the estate. His widowed sister moved back to the Court resumed her maiden name and struggled on with the running of the estate until after the Second World War, when it was broken up and the house sold.

Having examined the interior of the church it is now time to go for a stroll around the village to look at some of the interesting buildings and features that are mentioned in the *Diary*.

On leaving the church porch, turn left down the avenue of sturdy yew trees leading to the lychgate. Sadly the Wych elms of Kilvert's time have now gone. Near the chancel door in the south wall of the church is the tomb of Thomas Bridgewater. This was Kilvert's favourite tomb in the churchyard and he often used to sit on it deep in thought.

*After luncheon I spent a happy half hour in the lovely warm afternoon wandering about Clyro churchyard among the graves. I sat awhile on the old Catholic tomb of the 'Relict of Thomas Bridgewater' under the S. Church wall, near the chancel door. This is my favourite tomb. I love it better than all the tombs in the churchyard with its kindly 'Requiescat in pace', the prayer so full of peace, with its solemn remonder 'Tendimus huc omnes' and the simple Latin cross at the head of the inscription. There is something much more congenial to my mind in these old Catholic associations than in the bald ugly hideous accompaniments which too often mark the place of Protestant or rather Puritan burial. The Puritans of the last century seem to have tried to make the idea and place and associations of death and burial as gloomy, hideous and repulsive as possible, and they have most signally succeeded.*

*A small and irreverent spider came running swiftly towards me across the flat tombstone and scuttling over the sacred words and memories with most indecent haste and levity. Here it was very quiet and peaceful, nothing to disturb the stillness but the subdued village voices and the cawing of the rooks nesting and brooding in the tops of the high trees in the Castle clump. Somewhere near at hand I heard the innkeeper's voice behind the church and across the brook giving orders to a workman about planting some quick and privet.*

Near the lychgate can be found memorial stones to members of the Gore family who lived at Whitty's Mill on the Cabalva brook in a deep dingle below Crossway. The mill was in full working order when Kilvert wrote his diary and he tells us that the Gores were very well off. They made at least £200 a year which was very good money at that time. There were three daughters who all sadly died of consumption in their twenties.

This sundial stands in Clyro Churchyard and Kilvert tells us how he compared it with his watch in March 1871 *and they agreed most entirely*.

*I spent a happy half hour wandering about the Clyro Churchyard visiting the graves. I visited the new heavy and ambitious erection which Mrs Chaloner had put up to the memory of her husband Peter Chaloner.*

Near the south wall is this monument to Peter Chaloner who built Ashbrook House, where Kilvert lodged with his widow. Kilvert obviously thought that this *ambitious erection* was too grand a monument for a man of Peter Chaloner's position. Employed as a land agent for Clyro Court, he built Ty Dulas (Ashbrook House) where he lived with his wife, Mrs Arabella Chaloner. Their son Richard married Hannah Maria Dyke at Clyro Church in 1859.

The avenue of sturdy yews leading from the church porch to the lychgate

Row of 17th century cottages in Clyro

Directly opposite the lychgate is a row of 17th century cottages, which at the time of writing have not been modernised or spoilt in any way and would have looked very much the same in Kilvert's day.

Turn right here and walk towards the Post Office / Shop and then follow the road to the left to reach Ashbrook House (now The Kilvert Gallery). In Kilvert's time this house was known as Ty Dulas and a plaque on the outside wall near the entrance, records the fact that this was his home from 1865 to 1872. His sitting room was on the ground floor and his bedroom on the first floor, overlooking the street and opposite the Baskerville Arms.

The house was built in the 1850's by Peter Chaloner who also kept the The Swan ( now called the Baskerville Arms), directly opposite. He died in 1860 soon after the house was completed. His widow continued to live there for many years and made ends meet by taking in lodgers. The complete household during the seven years that Kilvert resided there would have consisted of Kilvert, Mrs Chaloner, her invalid daughter Elizabeth, a living-in maid and an additional lodger. This young gentleman was a solicitor's clerk from Hay who liked to have the occasional smoke and as Kilvert had a strong dislike of tobacco smoke they did not mix very much, even dining separately.

Ashbrook House in Kilvert's time was known as Ty Dulas and a plaque on the outside wall near the entrance, records the fact that this was his home from 1865 to 1872. His sitting room was on the ground floor and his bedroom on the first floor, overlooking the street and opposite the Baskerville Arms. The wall plaque of grey-green slate showing a profile of Kilvert in relief was unveiled in 1973 by the broadcaster, Wynford Vaughan Thomas, then President of the Kilvert Society.

The Kilvert Gallery was opened at Ashbrook House by the painter Elizabeth Organ in 1987, and visitors are made welcome. There is a small admission fee.

*Up early and working in my bedroom before breakfast. The swallows kept on dashing in at the open window and rustling round the room.*

The view from Kilvert's bedroom window towards a row of 17th century cottages

There appears to have been a limited supply of hot water in Ashbrook House for Kilvert used to take a cold bath in his bedroom every morning. On one occasion the water actually froze:

> *It was an intense frost. I sat down in my bath upon a sheet of ice which broke in the middle into large pieces while sharp points and jagged edges stuck all round the sides of the tub like chevaux de frise, not particularly comforting to the naked thigh and loins, for the keen ice cut like broken glass. The ice water stung and scorched like fire. I had to collect the floating pieces of ice and put them on a chair before I could use the sponge and then I had to thaw the sponge in my hands for it was a mass of ice.*

Directly opposite Ashbrook House is a little stone bridge spanning the Clyro Brook, which Kilvert variously refers to as Dulas Water and Clyro Water. The village women used to descend some steps beside this bridge to draw water. Kilvert comments how *the maidens and mothers go up and down the water steps, with their pitchers continually.*

The little stone bridge spanning the Clyro Brook

He also mentions how his brother *Perch went groping about in the brook and brought in a small crayfish which crawled about the table, horns, tail and claws like a fresh water clean brown lobster.*

Kilvert always referred to his brother, Edward as 'Teddy' or 'Perch'. He was born in 1849 and during his working life worked for the Inland Revenue subsequently becoming the Head Clerk at Somerset House.

Kilvert's sister, Dora

Edward Kilvert (Perch)

Just beyond the stone bridge is the *Baskerville Arms,* which was previously known as the *Swan* and when Kilvert looked across at it from his bedroom window, he always referred to it by this name, despite the fact that the name had been changed as long ago as 1848.

> *A wild rainy night. They are holding Clyro Feast Ball at the Swan opposite. As I write I hear the scraping and squealing of the fiddle and the ceaseless tramp of the dances as they stamp the floor in a country dance. An occasional blast of wind or rush of rain shakes my window.*

*The Swan Inn*, now known as the *Baskerville Arms* was re-named when the Baskerville family became owners of the Clyro estate. In Kilvert's day William Price was the innkeeper and in the 1871 census he is also described as a farmer.

> *Last night the Swan was very quiet, marvellously quiet and peaceful. No noise, rowing or fighting whatever and no men as there is sometimes are lying by the roadside all night, drunk, cursing, muttering and vomiting.*

Opposite the *Baskerville Arms* is a milestone which informs the traveller that Hay is just 1 mile 75 yards away. It also serves as a reminder that the main road used to pass through Clyro, until the village was by-passed by the A438 in the 1960s and the main street of the village returned to a reasonably peaceful existence.

The white three-storey building further on down the road was once a public house called *The New Inn*. It is now known as *New House* and stands at the foot of 'Cutter's Pitch' which is named after Mr Thomas who lived here and earned his living castrating lambs. Accordingly, he was known as 'Thomas the Cutter'.

This old milestone can be seen on the roadside opposite the *Baskerville Arms*

*New House* at the bottom of the road leading to Rhosgoch, was once a public house called the *New Inn*

In 1871 the inn lost its licence when the innkeeper was Elizabeth Morgan, a 35 year old Llowes woman, who is also described in the 1871 census as a grocer. Kilvert describes the sounds coming from the inn as he walked past, when a reception was being held there, celebrating the wedding of Catherine Price (of the New Inn) and a young Painscastle blacksmith called Davies:

> *As I passed the house I heard music and dancing. They were dancing in an upper room, unfurnished, tramp, tramp, tramp, to the jingling of a concertina. The stamping was tremendous. I thought they would have brought the floor down. They seemed to be jumping round and round. When I came back the dance seemed to have generated into a romp and the girls were squealing, as if they were being kissed or tickled and not against their will.*

Retrace your steps past the Post Office which retains its original shop window, and then walk on past Rose Cottage, an 18th century stone building. In the churchyard wall on the right you will see a ceramic memorial which marks the site of an old water outlet.

Follow the pavement up to the Painscastle Road and imagine Kilvert walking this way from Ty Dulas (Ashbrook House) to dine with the Rev Venables and his wife at the Vicarage.

> *How quiet and sunny the village was this evening as I went to the Vicarage to dinner. There was not a person in the roads or moving anywhere. The only living creature I saw was a dog.*

The yellow building on the left is Ty Melyn (Yellow House), and it is a medieval cruck-framed hall-house rebuilt in stone. Follow the road around to the left, passing Stocks House, which in Kilvert's day was the home of William Price who died at the age of 85. The house takes its name from the set of stocks that used to stand nearby.

> *Sally (Whitney) said she remembered the old Clyro stocks and whipping post which stood by the village pound in front of their door. She had often seen people in the stocks and once she saw a sweep whipped by a parish constable for using foul language at the Swan. When people were put in the stocks it was generally for rioting and using bad language at the Swan and fighting.*

On the corner of the old main road is Stock House, which takes its name from a set of stocks which used to stand nearby

This roughcast, twin-gabled house with tall chimneys of local stone is the Old Vicarage where the Venables family lived and Kilvert was a regular visitor

Kilvert also mentions the stocks when he tells how *a drunken fellow named James Davies was put in the stocks by Archdeacon Venables and the parish constable, Jim's friend later 'brought an axe and beat the stocks to pieces and let the poor prisoner out. The two worthies fled away to Hereford... Clyro people, seeing the stocks broken, demolished and burnt the stocks and whipping post, and no one was ever confined or whipped at Clyro after that.*

Shortly on the right will be seen the *Old Vicarage*, which Kilvert knew as the home of the Rev Richard Lester Venables and his family. When Kilvert first came to Clyro, the Vicar was a widower but subsequently married Agnes Minna, youngest daughter of Henry Shepherd Pearson, by whom he had one son (who died in 1876) and two daughters, Katharine Minna and Caroline Emily. Two small bungalows have been built on what used to be the front lawn of the old vicarage.

Cross the road to walk past the bus shelter and follow the pavement leading past the drive to Cae Mawr (private residence). This white Regency style house is beautifully situated on the hillside opposite Clyro School, Cae Mawr (Big Field) was built in 1805 by the Rev Doctor William Powell. When he died the house and estate were sold to the Baskerville family who lived there until the new Clyro Court was completed. The house is approached by a long driveway and from its grounds the occupants enjoy a panoramic view of the Wye Valley and Black Mountains. Cae Mawr was the home of Hopewell Morrell who was probably Kilvert's best friend during his time in Clyro. He originally came from Forthampton, Gloucestershire and despite the fact that he was seven years younger than Kilvert, he was a Medical Officer of Health of the Hay District and also a magistrate.

> *Called at Cae Mawr at 3.30 and found Mr and Mrs Morrell playing croquet with his sister and Miss Morrell of Moulsford who are staying in the house, having returned with him on Tuesday. Joined them and we had two merry games. The two eldest Miss Baskervilles came in by the wicket gate while we were playing and we had tea on the lawn. I stayed to dinner. After dinner we had archery.*

The Rev Richard Lester Venables, Vicar of Clyro

Mrs Venables, the Vicar's second wife

The old Clyro Village School where Kilvert taught daily, teaching the three Rs and the Catechism. Virtually every child in the parish between the ages of four and twelve attended the school.

Cross the main road with care and keep straight on following the pavement to pass on your right the old village school. Within these walls, Kilvert once taught the three R's and the catechism daily to children from around the parish between the ages of 4 and 12. It was here that he once lost his heart to ten-year old Gipsy Lizzie (Elizabeth Jones) who the 1871 Census reveals, was born at Pontypool in Monmouthshire. Her grandfather was John Harris of Pen-y-cae.

> *How is the indescribable beauty of that most lovely face to be described - the dark soft curls parting back from the pure white transparent brow, the exquisite little mouth and pearly tiny teeth, the pure straight delicate features, the long dark fringes and white eyelids that droop over and curtain her eyes, when they are cast down or bent upon her book, and seem to rest upon that soft clear cheek, and when the eyes are raised, that clear unfathomable blue depth of wide wonder and enquiry and unsullied and unsuspecting innocence. Oh child, child, if you did but know your own power!*

Across to the left is Castle Estate Road which takes its name from the tree-clad knoll which Kilvert refers to as ***Castle Clump and is the site of Clyro Castle.***This lordship was in the de Braose territories but was later held by the Baskervilles, who built a strong keep on the mound which in 1403, during the time of Henry IV, was recorded as a defensible stronghold. At the time of writing, Clyro Community Council are planning to clear trees and undergrowth from the mound to make it visible and accessible.

Continue past *Pottery Cottage* and follow the pavement beside the Hay Road to reach a finger post on the right. Just below this point, on the left side of the road used to be a large pool which Kilvert refers to as *Peter's Pool*. It was named after St Peter, the Patron Saint of fishermen. Go through a gate and follow a broad track above a sloping field enjoying a fine view towards the Black Mountains. Shortly, go through another gate and head across a field to a stile. On the left you will see a section of the old main road which now forms the entrance drive to Clyro Court Farm.

Cross the main road with care, go diagonally left of the stile, and then turn left along the pavement. On the other side of the main road you will see a large Gothic arch piercing a stone wall. This was once the entrance to Old Clyro Court, a lovely Elizabethan manor, standing in a spacious park on the site of a monastic grange belonging to the Cistercian Abbey Cwmhir. The manor house was built by the Vaughan family of Bredwardine, who at one time owned much of Clyro. In 1580 it was the home of Roger Vaughan, High Sheriff of Radnorshire and a descendant of Einion Clud, Lord of Elfael. Many years ago this grand house was badly damaged by fire and it is now just a farmhouse. In Kilvert's time the road passing the entrance arch had a reputation of being haunted.

Follow the pavement and then a wide grass verge down to the long drive leading to Baskerville Court Hotel. Of interest is the colourful sign depicting the famous fictional detective, Sherlock Holmes, complete with deerstalker and pipe. This relates to the time when the famous author Sir Arthur Conan Doyle stayed there whilst researching for his story entitled *'The Hound of the Baskervilles'*. It is said that the Baskerville family allowed him to use their name with the proviso that the story was set somewhere else. Inspiration possibly came from the local legend concerning a wicked member of that family who was once chased by a gigantic hound. Sir Arthur Conan Doyle of course set his story on Dartmoor and it became a best seller.

Clyro Court was built in the 1840s for Thomas Mynors Baskerville. In Kilvert's time it was the home of the young Baskerville Squire who lived in this grand house with his two unmarried brothers, three unmarried sisters and about eight servants. After the Second World War Clyro Court was sold to Radnorshire District Council to become a Secondary Modern School. In the early 1970s it became a hotel and health farm. It changed hands again in 1984 and was re-named Baskerville Hall Hotel.

*We went to a croquet party at Clyro Court... The party divided between croquet and archery. We had a long well-fought game of eight, too evenly matched to be finished in the time, so it was drawn. The players were Miss Oswald, Miss M. Morrell, Baskerville and Perch against Miss Edith Baskerville, Alice and Fanny Bevan and myself. The shooters were the other two Miss Baskervilles, the Crichtons, the other three Morrells, Mary Bevan and Miss Marion Bailey of Easton...*

Walk up the long drive to see the grand mansion which Kilvert knew as Clyro Court and was frequently entertained here by members of the Baskerville family.

A special feature inside the house is the high colonnaded entrance hall leading to a grand ceremonial staircase which sweeps up to the landings and is lit by a glass dome in the roof.

Just outside the village, near the junction of the A4153 and B4351, opposite the old school, is a tree-clad knoll, known by Kilvert as Castle Clump, on which a de Braose built a motte and bailey castle and a Baskerville erected a stone keep.

This impressive Gothic arch was once the entrance to Old Clyro Court, an Elizabethan manor which was sadly damaged by fire many years ago and is now just a farmhouse.

*The trees blazed with the diamonds of the melting hoar frost. The wet village roads shone like silver and the market folk thronged past the Vicarage and School.... How indescribable was that lovely brilliant variegated scene. A rook shot up out of the valley and towered above the silver mist into the bright blue sky over the golden oaks, rising against the dark blue mountains still patched and ribbed with snow.*

## Walk 1 - Kilvert's Clyro

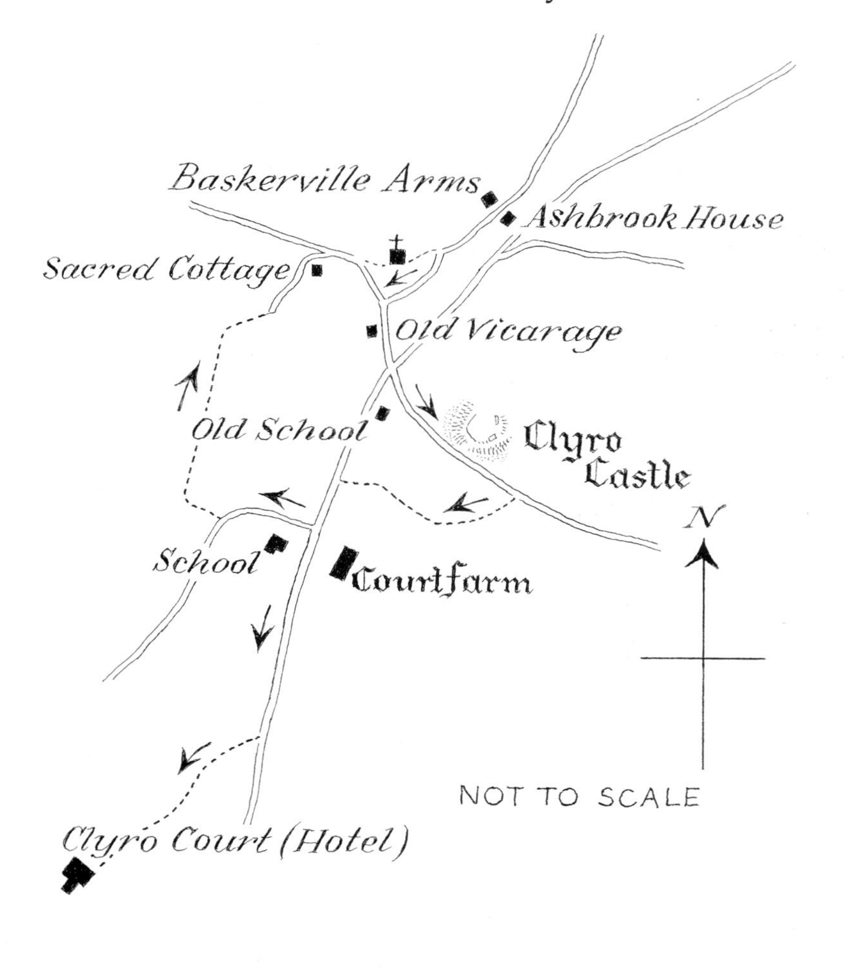

Sacred Cottage can be found in the lane leading up to the old walled garden behind Cae Mawr. It is one of the oldest houses in Clyro and was at one time the vicarage. In Kilvert's day it was the home of Esther Rogers, a widow in her sixties and her two grown-up sons, Thomas and James. She told Kilvert how her brother had been killed by a French lancer at Waterloo. She remembered him as a tall young man wearing a scarlet uniform mounted on a black horse with white legs.

Now walk back up the long drive and return along the grass verge. On reaching a road coming down from the left you now have a choice. Either continue along the pavement back to Clyro village or complete a circuit as follows:

Go up the road, passing Clyro Primary School, which was built on a corner of the Clyro Court grounds some years ago to replace the old village school. The land on which the new school stands was known as 'The Cherry Orchard' in Kilvert's time. Follow the road up hill and just after it bends to the left, go through a small metal gate on the right, near a house called 'Little Cedars'. Follow the left edge of the garden up to a little wooden gate. Then go right to pass between the fence and a large oak tree, to reach a gate. Go straight across the next field to reach another gate. Then turn right down a broad sunken track leading down to the bottom right hand corner of the field. Go over a stile beside a gate and on reaching a surfaced lane turn left. Soon the tower of Clyro Church will come into view and the lane leads on down past *Sacred Cottage*, which was the first Vicarage. Kilvert knew it as the home of Esther Rogers.

On meeting the Painscastle Road, turn right along the pavement, then cross the road and go through a kissing gate to enter the churchyard.

A row of military-like crosses commemorating members of the Baskerville family

Near the stone wall at this end of the churchyard will be found a row of Baskerville graves arranged in a military fashion. The five crosses, reading from left to right commemorate:-

Edith Meliora Sybil Baskerville - Born 1846 Died 1916

Clara Anne Maria Baskerville - Born 1848 Died 1901

Gertrude Alice Elizabeth Baskerville - Born 1844 Died 1895

Edward Reginald Mynors Baskerville - Born 1843 Died 1916

Herbert Witherstone Mynors Baskerville - Born 1841 Died 1926

Just in front of these graves is a tall stone cross commemorating successive heads of the family. There are four tomb chests at its foot, but three of them bear no inscription. The dynasty ended with the death of Ralph Hopton Baskerville who was killed in the Great War.

The name of Baskerville is on the roll of Battle Abbey. This family originated from Bacqueville, near Rouen and they settled in this area soon after the Conquest with their seat at Eardisley. They intermarried with the first families in the county, served the office of High Sheriff, no less than 21 times, and were elected knights of the Shire in eleven Parliaments.

Walter Thomas Baskerville married on 18th November 1875, Bertha Maria (b.1847 d.1892), only surviving daughter of John Hopton of Cannon Frome Court, Herefordshire. He died on 29th August 1897 and his son Ralph Hopton (b. February 13th, 1883) succeeded to the property upon his coming of age in 1904. His sisters were Sybil Maude (b. February 1st 1877) and Dorothy Nest (b. January 11th 1880).

In the bottom corner of the churchyard by the main gate is the village war memorial to men who died in the Great War. Heading the list is Captain Ralph Hopton Baskerville.

## WALK 2
### *South of Clyro*
2 ½ miles (4km)

*I strolled down the lane till I came in sight of the full mill pond shining between the willow trunks like a lake of indefinite size. Here and there the banks and road sides were spangled with primroses and they shone like stars among the little brakes and bramble thickets overhanging the brook. A sheep and lamb having broken bounds were wandering about the lane by themselves and kept on fording and refording the brook where it crosses the road to get out of my way. The mill was silent except for the splash of water from 'the dark dripping wheel.' The mill pond was full, but I forgot to look at the sun in it to see if he was dancing as he is said to do on Easter morning.*

Rev Francis Kilvert

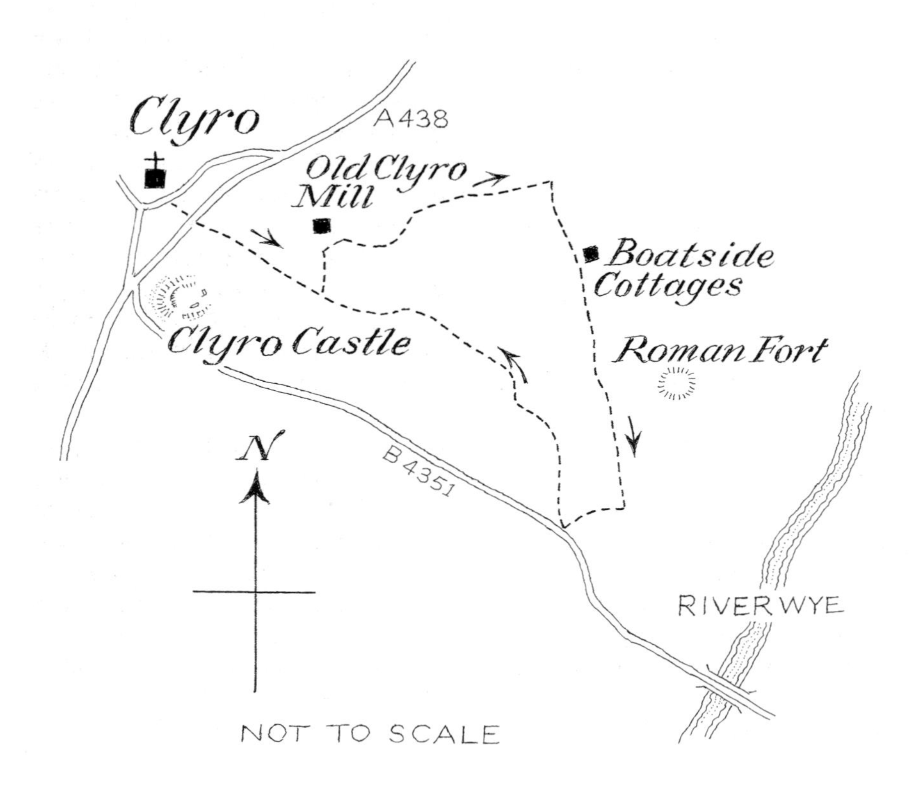

Walk down the lane between Ashbrook House (The Kilvert Gallery) and the Post Office. It was in this lane that Hannah Whitney's cottage was situated. Kilvert often used to sit there with her ***talking*** *about old times and listening to her reminiscences and tales of the dear old times, the simple primitive times in Bryngwyn nearly ninety years ago*. Kilvert on August 28th, 1878 made a return visit to Clyro and observed that: *Old Hannah Whitney's Cottage, at the door of which she used to sit knitting so cheerfully in mob cap, crossover shawl and spectacles, is alas pulled down*.

Cross the main road with care and go a short way down the drive leading to Clyro Mill ( now called 'Kilvert's Mill ), which was powered by the Dulas brook. Go over a stile on the right and follow a path straight on through the field. After crossing a ridge of higher ground you will meet a fence. At the end of the fence follow a waymarked path to the left towards the renovated mill. Keep the fence on your left to reach a stile in the corner of the field. Go straight on through the next field, walking beside a fence to reach another stile.

Bear slightly right across the next field to pass through a gap in the trees and between two gate posts. Then bear slightly right up through the next field to reach a stile and a finger post. After rain a small pond forms in the hollow at the bottom of this field. Pause at the stile to look back at Clyro in its delightful setting beneath the backcloth of wooded hills.

Now turn right along a tarmac lane, passing Boatside Cottages on the left. On the higher ground directly above here is the site of a Roman camp which was built in about 50 AD and covers an area of 26 acres, large enough to accommodate an entire legion. It was never replaced by a permanent stone-built fort and was occupied only during the Conquest. A Roman road ran to it from Magnis near Credenhill. In Roman times there was a ford below the Clyro camp across the Wye. Legend has it that the XX Legion was ambushed here and virtually destroyed by the Silurian warriors.

In due course the view opens up and when the road bends to the right, Hay Castle can be seen dominating the town. Just before you join the B4351, turn sharp right through a gate. Follow the driveway (leading to Radnor's End Camping Site) for a short distance to reach another gate. Then keep straight on beside a hedge, through the next field. Go over a stile on the left in the corner of the field. Head straight across the next field bearing very slightly right to reach a stile beside a gate. Below now is Tir-mynach Farm. The name translates as 'Monk-land' and the estate probably constituted Clyro Grange, a part of the property with which the Abbey of Cwmhir was endowed.

View across the fields towards Clyro

Go straight across the next field with Clyro Church now directly ahead. Walk through the next field keeping the hedge on your right to reach a stile in the bottom right hand corner near two gates.

Head across the next field, keeping diagonally left. Make for the stile in the bottom right corner of the field. Then head directly towards Clyro to rejoin your outward route.

> *When I looked at the dear old village nestling round the Church in the hollow at the dingle mouth and saw the fringes of the beautiful woods and the hanging orchards and the green slopes of Penllan and the white farms and cottages dotted over the hills a thousand sweet and sad memories came over me and all my heart rose up within me and went out in love towards the beloved place and people among whom I lived so long and happily.*

## *Clyro Mill*

*The Western wind blew wild and chill,*
*There came a sound of distant rain,*
*As loitering down the winding lane*
*We passed above the bustling mill,*

*Along the willow-shaded pond,*
*Between the wheel and water-grate,*
*And through the swinging wicket gate,*
*To sunny fields that slope beyond;*

*Down to a way-worn mouldering stile,*
*And path that skirts the headland edge,*
*Beneath a hollow eldern hedge;*
*And as the sun broke to a smile,*

*We paused upon a rising hill,*
*To mark the windings of a brook,*
*And all the air around us shook*
*With throbbings of the booming mill.*

Rev Francis. Kilvert

## WALK 3

### *Above Clyro*

$1\frac{1}{2}$ miles ( 2.4 km)

Follow the Painscastle Road out of Clyro, along the pavement, passing Begwyns Bluff on the left. In Kilvert's time this housing estate would have been just green fields and no doubt he would be amazed to see how this village has grown in size.

The large house called Pentwyn which Kilvert knew as the home of Miss Emma Bynon, is passed on the right. When John Wesley visited Radnorshire he often stayed in this house and according to Canon W.E.T. Morgan (*Woolhope Transactions* 1923) the stone on which he stood was removed to Paradise Cottage.

At the point where the road narrows, follow a signposted footpath to the right. It passes above a tennis court and leads down into the bottom of the valley. Ignore the wide footbridge on the right and keep straight on to shortly cross a narrow bridge spanning the Clyro Brook which chatters musically down through this beautiful dingle.

The path leads on up through the trees and soon leaves the side of the stream to ascend to a stile on the right. It then rises more steeply between a fence and a gully. At the top of the slope, which Kilvert called *Jacob's Ladder*, go over a stile and enter a field. Pause here to catch your breath and enjoy the view south of Clyro.

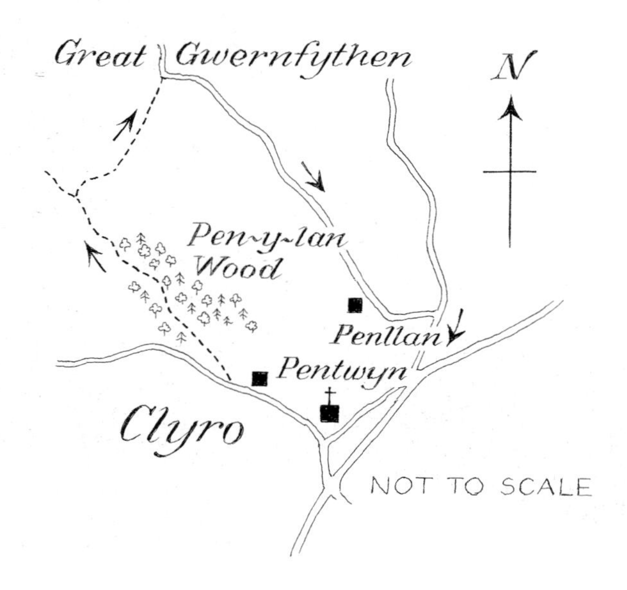

On 19th August, 1870 Kilvert commented how he saw *Ben Lloyd of the Cwm Bryngwyn reeling up the steep fields above Jacob's Ladder carrying a horse collar and butter tub. Just as I came up the drunken man fell sprawling on his back. He got up looking foolish and astonished...*

Continue up the field keeping the fence and wood on your right. In due course the gradient becomes less steep. Go through a small wooden gate at the top of the field and then through a gate on the right to follow a cart track. Some stepping stones have been provided on a particularly muddy patch.

The track becomes less distinct but continue through the next field to reach another gate. Then cross the next field, making for a gate in a hedge. From there go diagonally up to the top right hand corner of the next field to reach a gate just below Great Gwernfythen Farm. Now turn right down the road leading past Penllan Farm, with the Black Mountains dominating the view ahead.

At the bottom of the hill turn right at the T-junction and head back to Clyro, passing the old 'New Inn' on the left.

# WALK 4
## *To Hay-on-Wye*
1 ¼ miles ( 1.98 km)

*I walked to Hay. The afternoon was brilliant in its loveliness. The sun was under a cloud from behind which streamed seven broad rays on to the variegated mountain and valley, river and meadow, striking out brilliant gems of sunlit emerald green on the hillsides*

Rev Francis Kilvert

Walk down the lane between Ashbrook House (The Kilvert Gallery) and the Post Office. Cross the main road with care and go a short way down the drive leading to Clyro Mill (now called 'Kilvert's Mill ). Go over a stile on the right and follow a path straight on through the field. After crossing a ridge of slightly higher ground you will meet a fence.

From the end of the fence continue straight up to the top left corner of the field where the stile is concealed from view. Keep straight on through the next field to reach a stile to the left of double gates. Follow the left hedge and fence around the next field to reach a stile in the hedge to the right of a gate. Then pass through a field above Tyr Mynach Farm to reach a stile beside a gate. Bear diagonally right across the next field to a stile in the top corner. Follow the hedge down to the right to a gate and the drive of Radnor's End Camping Site.

On meeting the main road turn left and follow it to Hay-on-Wye.

*I strolled back to Clyro by the fields in time for the funeral from Newchurch at 3 o' clock. It was delicious strolling across the sunny breezy fields with the world of beauty lying all around, the light blue mountains and the green valley, and the grey clusters of a town canopied by blue smoke, the long line of variegated banks and hills dotted with white cottages and the beautiful village at the dingle mouth.*

## Walk 4 - To Hay-on-Wye

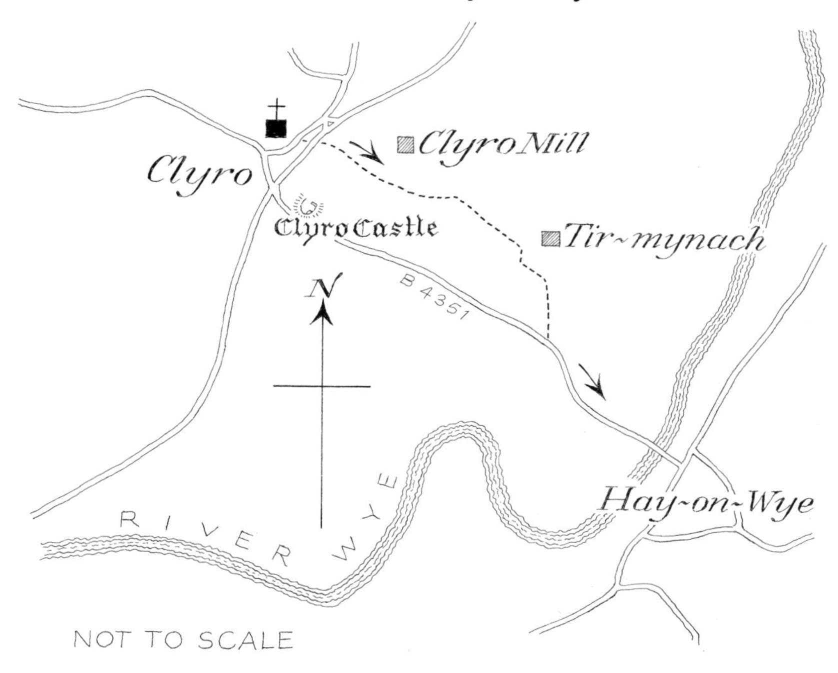


## HAY-ON-WYE

*I had the satisfaction of managing to walk from Hay to Clyro by the fields without meeting a single person, always a great triumph to me and a subject for warm self congratulation for I have a peculiar dislike to meeting people, and a peculiar liking for a deserted road.*

Rev Francis Kilvert

The name Hay is an anglicised form of the old Norman-French name La Haie, meaning 'the enclosure', while the Welsh name of Y Gelli or in full Y Gelli Gandryll means 'the broken grove'. In Kilvert's time the town was known as Hay. The addition of '-on-Wye' was proposed by a one-time postmaster of the town who got fed up with letters going astray to Hay in the Orkneys. In 1947 the name was accordingly changed by the resolution of the Urban District Council, but the railway station name did not appear as Hay-on-Wye in the public time tables until June, 1955.

Hay Railway Station

It is interesting that when the railway was in operation the town was largely in Wales while the station platform was in England, the dividing line being the Dulas Brook which flowed into the Wye at the west end of the platform. There was a time when the Welsh and English would have glowered at each other across the Dulas Brook, and both sides were never slow at rustling sheep or cattle which strayed too near the border. In order to keep everyone satisfied the town artificially divided into two parts - English Hay and Welsh Hay, but attitudes are very different today, with visitors coming from all parts of the world.

Hay is internationally known for its bookshops, each one specialising in new and secondhand books to suit all tastes. Even the town's cinema has been converted into a multi-tiered book-store containing thousands of volumes.

Dominating the town, at its highest point, are the remains of Hay Castle which include a 13th century gateway and a length of walling which are adjoined by a 17th century Jacobean mansion built by James Boyle of Hereford. During Kilvert's time this was the home of the Vicar of Hay, the Rev William Latham Bevan, who leased the building from his wealthy uncle Sir Joseph Bailey, the retired ironmaster who resided at Glanusk, near Crickhowell. Kilvert was a regular visitor to Hay Castle, where he was warmly welcomed by the Bevan family, whose home was a centre of social life in the town and a noted venue for croquet and archery.

An archery group at Hay Castle in about 1880

The archery contests took place in the field below the castle which is now the site of a large car park, established to cope with the ever-growing number of visitors that now come to the town. It was a very different scene in Kilvert's day:

> *The ladies sat watching under the trees while the arrows flashed past with a whistling rush and the glorious afternoon sunlight shone mellow upon the bushes, and the still soft air of the river valley was filled with the cooing of woodpigeons and the strange mournful cry of the moorhen and dab chicks....*

It was in Hay Castle one day, that Kilvert heard from Mr Bevan that Cambridge had won the boat race. Kilvert, who was himself an Oxford man generously remarked, *I am very glad and I think that most people will be, Oxford or not.* This remark was made because Oxford had won the race for the last nine years!

Kilvert made regular visits to Hay, usually on foot and very often as much as three or four times a week. For him it was an exciting place for virtually everything that he needed could be obtained there. He tells for example, how on the 11th of February, 1870 he made his way from Clyro across the fields to Hay after breakfast. At 9.00 am he crossed the bridge and paid a visit to Bevan the watchmaker who repaired his broken musical box. He then bought four valentines (cards) at Horden's and ordered cheese at Hadley's.

Three days later he returned to Hay on St Valentine's Day, walking to town with his Vicar to look at bedding in Williams the draper. This was intended for the poor of Clyro and was purchased out of surplus Communion Alms.

It was also at Horden's (currently a boutique called 'Elenbach') in Castle Street, that Kilvert purchased his writing paper and those vital notebooks in which he wrote his diary.

Hay is a market town with narrow winding streets and interesting buildings. Richard Booth the self-proclaimed 'King of Hay' is responsible for putting the place on the map as a world famous centre for people who love books.

## WALK 5
## Around Hay-on-Wye

¾ miles (1.2km)

Start from the parking area in front of Hay Castle

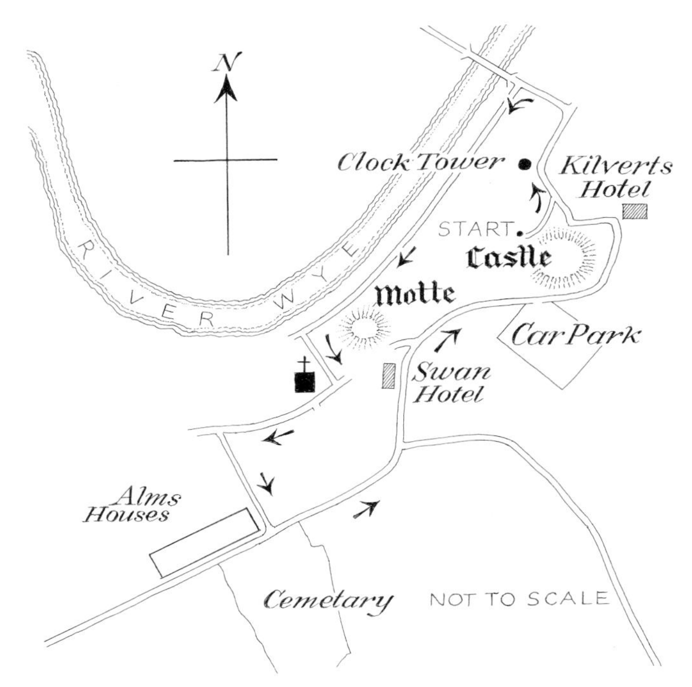


With your back to the castle, look up to see a sculptured figure of Henry VII (Henry Tudor, 1485-1509), high on the building to your right. It is the work of Edward Folkard and was put there in March 1995. The building to which it is fastened is the Town Hall which was built on the site of an older one erected in the reign of James I. The present building dates from1840 and the lower part was formerly used as a cheese market.

Go down the street (High Town) below the Town Hall and turn left between a chemist shop and a bookshop, following a pedestrianised lane. Walk past the elegant clock tower (erected in 1884 by J. C. Hadden of Hereford at a cost of £600. Part of this sum was raised by a bazaar. Cross Broad Street and follow the pavement to the right, past the *Rose & Crown* Inn to turn left down Bridge Street by the *Three Tuns* Inn, which is a 16th century timber-framed building. Apart from the Castle it is the oldest building in Hay.

The Jacobean house which is linked to the remnants of the old Norman Castle was the home of the Bevan family who lived there during Kilvert's time. He was a frequent visitor to their home, discussing church matters, enjoying croquet on the lawn, followed by tea and strawberries and cultured conversation with friends who regularly met one another at local mansions. When Archdeacon Bevan retired in 1902, his successor the Rev J. A. Smith also used the castle as a 'vicarage' for the two years that he was in Hay.

**History of Hay Castle**

1100 Walter Revel built the first motte and bailey castle
1200 William de Braose II built a new castle
1233 Castle rebuilt by Henry III
1236 Town walls built
1264 Castle captured by Prince Edward
1265 Damaged by Simon de Montfort, Earl of Leicester
1322 Captured by the King's forces and confiscated by the Crown
1402 Sacked by Owain Glyndwr
1460 Castle in a ruined state
1620 Jacobean mansion built
1833 Joseph Bailey (knighted in 1852) became Lord of the Manor
1845 Castle leased by Joseph Bailey to Rev W. L. Bevan

The *Rose and Crown* gets a mention, when in April 1870, Kilvert noticed:

> *Phillips of Pen y Llan standing at the door...I asked Phillips why he never came to church. He said he had not been for a year because he had heard that I had said he was wrong in fighting in public houses. I told him I could not remember exactly what I had said a year ago, but I was not afraid to tell him to his face that he was wrong in fighting and rowing. He seemed rather pleased and promised to come to church next Sunday.*

Kilvert visited the *Rose and Crown* when he attended the annual Book Club sale. He would have been enthralled by the many bookshops that can be found in the town today and of great interest to him would also be the present day annual Hay Festival, the status and reputation of which grows each year.

Just before the bridge over the Wye, go right down a path leading to a picnic area. Pass under the road bridge and continue left along the old railway line which is now a cycle route established by Sustrans.

> *The river swollen by yesterday's rain was tumbling and rushing brown and tumultuous under Hay Bridge and sweeping round the curves below where the yellowing trees leaned over the brown water hurrying along the winding shore.*

The first bridge which had five stone arches and was 16 feet below the present level, was completed in 1763 when a 90 year lease of tolls was granted to the builders. It at last meant that the dangerous crossing by ferry was no longer necessary, but in February 1795, the bridge was swept away by a flood which also destoyed the bridges at Glasbury and Whitney. Only two arches on the Radnorshire side remained standing and these were subsequently connected to the Hay bank by means of two wooden piers.

In 1838 the bridge was described as being *'in a very dilapidated state.'* It was badly damaged in February 1855 when masses of ice swept away the wooden portion. Repairs were again carried out and ten years later the bridge was described as *'...a crazy old structure, spliced, propped and patched in all directions, with dangerous approaches on each side, with a short steep pitch with a tramroad crossing at the bottom, and on the other side of the tramroad, the bridge gate.'*

In 1864 a new bridge at a higher level was completed at a cost of about £7,000. It was a lattice girder construction, 388 feet long with the roadway 16 feet above the level of the old bridge. This was replaced by the present bridge in 1958.

Hay-on-Wye at the turn of the 20th century with the old river bridge carrying the road to Clyro in the background

The pleasant leafy track running parallel with the river provides a good opportunity to get away from the busy streets of Hay for a while. The only sounds are bird song and water music. Below the old railway is a riverside path known as 'Bailey's Walk'. It was laid out in 1884 by Sir Joseph Bailey at his own expense and he also built the Town Hall. In 1897 to commemorate Queen Victoria's Jubilee, the walk was extended from the river bridge to Wyeford Road.

On reaching a point below the church, go left up a path (signposted Town Centre), leading up above a dingle with the churchyard wall on the right. Go through a gate to reach a pavement and the entrance gate to St Mary's Church. To the left can be seen a large grass covered mound, all that remains of the original castle.

Situated between the town and the church is a large motte (GR 226422), the original castle, known as 'Castello de haia' which was built by the Norman knight, Walter Revell in about 1100. It adjoins Gypsy Lane and is known by Hay folk as 'The Tump'.

The parish church of St Mary (GR 225422) is situated towards the east end of the town, overlooking the river. It was rebuilt (except for the tower) in the 19th century and a strange feature inside is the quasi-Moorish arcade which separates the nave from the chancel.

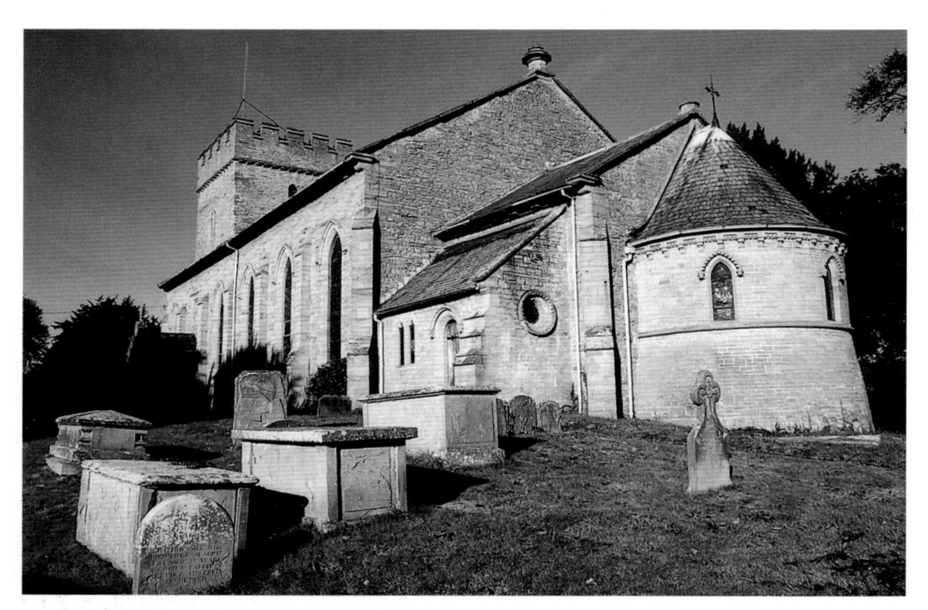

St Mary's Church is rather a plain building which was much restored in 1867. It consists of a nave and tower, together with an apsidal chancel which was added at the Restoration. Inside can be seen memorial brasses commemorating the Bevan family who in Kilvert's time resided in Hay Castle. This church is mentioned many times in the *Diary* and in one memorable entry, Kilvert describes how shocked he was to see Mrs Crichton sitting in the church listening to the same sermon that she would have heard him preaching in Clyro Church that afternoon.

In 1739 the peal of six bells was taken down and sent by river boat to the Evans foundry at Chepstow for re-casting. There is a story that either on the outward or the return journey, five of the bells were by some means lost. This may have given rise to the legend that the bells are in Steeple Pool which is a deep and dangerous part of the Wye below Bailey Walk.

Kilvert frequently officiated in this church on Sundays and weekdays, even though the vicar Rev William Latham Bevan, had a curate, Arthur Jones.

After visiting the church, walk from the porch to the main gate and turn right along the pavement, beside the churchyard wall. Then opposite a childrens' play area, cross the road and turn left, following a narrow path between a fence and the play area. On reaching a metal kissing gate turn left along the pavement beside the main road. Soon you will pass on the left the Harley Almshouses. An inscription records that: 'These Almshouses were built and endowed by Frances Harley, in memory of her sister Martha Harley of Trebarried in 1836. They were modernised in 1974'.

The Harley Almshouses on the Brecon road, where Kilvert observed that *'daffodils were nodding in bright yellow clumps in garden plots before the almshouses doors.'* They were erected in 1836 by Miss Frances Harley of Trebarried in memory of her sister. She reserved to herself during her lifetime the right to nominate the almswomen and to manage the charity, endowing it with two farms. These were to produce an annual rent of £100, of which £10 was to be paid into a repairs and insurance fund and £15 annually to be paid to each of the inmates. An upper storey was later built above the two middle houses to provide accomodation for a matron. In one of the houses once resided Mrs Esther Price, aged 69, from Colva whom Kilvert mentions in his *Diary*.

Cross the road to visit Hay Cemetery, which Kilvert mentions was opened and dedicated by the Right Reverend Charles Alford, Bishop of Victoria, Hong Kong on 20th July, 1870. Go through the lychgate and walk most of the way up the central avenue to reach two seats. Behind the one on the left is an intricately carved Celtic cross marking the grave of the Rev William Latham Bevan, Archdeacon of Brecon, Canon of St David's and for 56 years Vicar of this parish. He was born on May 1st, 1821 and died August 2nd 1908. The cross also commemorates his wife Louisa who was born in 1820 and died in 1908.

This fine Celtic Cross erected in 1908, dedicated to the Rev William Latham Bevan and his wife Louisa. The Rev William Latham Bevan was born in 1820 at Beaufort, the son of William Hibbs Bevan of Glannant, Crickhowell and Margaret, daughter of Joseph Latham of Broughton and Crickhowell. He was educated at Rugby and Hereford College, Oxford, and ordained in London.

In 1845 he became Vicar of Hay at the age of 25, through the patronage of his uncle, Sir Joseph Bailey, who had married William's maternal aunt as his first wife. He was to hold this living for 56 years and even declined four deaneries in Wales, preferring to remain in his parish. Not only did Bevan do a vast amount of restoration work on the parish church but he also paid for the building of the parish hall out of his own pocket. He established the British School in the town and built the clock tower. William married Louisa, daughter of Tomkyns Dew in 1849. Their marriage was a long and happy one and they had four sons.

From 1876-79 he was prebendary of Llandewi-Aberarth in St David's Cathedral and Canon of St David's 1870-93. In 1880 he was made Proctor of the Diocese of St David's, a position he held until 1895. Then, at the age of 75, he was appointed Archdeacon of Brecon, a position which did not require him to move from Hay. He resigned his living at Hay-on-Wye in 1901 after fifty-six years and retired to the Ely Tower, Brecon. This became the Bishop's Palace and his son Edward Latham Bevan was to be consecrated first Bishop of Brecon and Swansea in 1923.

William Latham Bevan died in Brecon on 28th August, 1908 and was buried in Hay Cemetery. The Diocesan conference at St David's in 1908 decided to establish a memorial to him and two years later, in St Mary's Church, Hay-on-Wye, the family memorial, consisting of a marble chancel pavement and carved oak choir stalls was unveiled.

Rev William Latham Bevan, Vicar of Hay

Mrs Louisa Bevan

Edward Latham Bevan, the son of William Latham Bevan appears in the *Diary* as little Teddy Bevan who occasionally went for walks with Kilvert. He became first Bishop of Swansea and Brecon and died at Weymouth in 1934, bequeathing the greater part of his personal fortune to Brecon Cathedral. This included £10,000 to the upkeep of the Cathedral and £2,000 for the Cathedral choir. In the Cathedral is a recumbent bronze figure of him by Sir Goscombe John RA.

Return down the avenue and turn right along the pavement to pass the mountain road to Capel-y-ffin. On the left now will be seen a second set of almshouses. The inscription reads: *'These Almshouses were erected and endowed by Frances Harley to the memory of her mother the Hon Mrs Harley of Trebarried for the reception of six poor indigent women AD MDCCCXXXII.'*

The Lyne family used to stay at the *Swan Hotel* when they were visiting Joseph Leycester Lyne (Father Ignatius) at Capel-y-ffin. In the 1870's the brother of Father Ignatius used to keep twenty-two dogs in a stone barn at the rear of the hotel.

Continue past the *Swan Hotel* and follow the main street, passing the *Blue Boar Inn* on the right, at the corner of Castle Street and Oxford Road. Here, Good Friday 1870, Kilvert was shocked to see *a party of gentlemen in white waistcoats etc... bent on a day's pleasure*. Only a few weeks earlier an inquest had been held at the *Blue Boar* following the suicide of the barmaid, who had thrown herself into the Wye at Glasbury.

Opposite 'Elenbach' (6, Castle Street) which in Kilvert's day was a stationery shop called Horden's, go up an alley way on the right, passing some bookshops to reach the Bredwardine road. Turn left along the pavement to walk beside the perimeter wall of Hay Castle. Then turn left down Oxford Terrace to pass on the right Salem Baptist Chapel which was established in 1649, rebuilt in 1878 and can claim to be the second oldest Nonconformist Chapel in Wales. It was founded shortly after the parent church at Ilston in Gower by John Miles. In February 1650, Baptists from the Olchon, Llanigon and Hay districts were united in a closed-communion Baptish church centred on Hay. The schoolroom is in its original form and is probably the oldest in Wales still in existence.

Continue down 'the Bullring' to reach *Kilvert's Hotel* which makes an appropriate finishing point to this walk A turning on the left leads back to your starting point below the Castle, just a short distance away.

*Kilvert's Hotel* makes a suitable ending to this walk

There have been at least 35 inns and hotels in Hay and the following are given as examples:-

Seven Stars Inn, Bridge End, The Lamb, The Ship, Tanner's Arms, Three Tuns, Black Swan, Rose and Crown, Old White Lion, King's Head, Old Mitre, Wheatsheaf, Castle, Half Moon, New Inn, Black Lion, Drovers Arms, The Bear, The Bell, Three Horseshoes, Market Tavern, The Fountain, Mason's Arms, Blue Boar, Wine Vaults, The Cock, Golden Lion, The Dog Inn (later The Talbot), The Grapes, The George, White Swan Hotel, Bunch of Grapes, Sun Inn, New Sun Inn and The Royal Oak.

# CAR TOUR TO LLANIGON

6 ¼ miles (10 km)

Take the Brecon road (B4350) out of Hay and shortly turn left for Llanigon (signposted Llanigon 1 ½ miles and Felindre 4 miles). On reaching Llanigon, ignore the first turning left and bear left at the next junction to reach **St Eigon's Church** (GR 214399). Park by the lychgate just above the church or in front of St Eigon's Villas.

**Llanigon** was originally known as Thomaschirche which later took the Welsh form of Llanthomas. This is an unusual church for on the outside it resembles a large barn.

In Kilvert's time the vicar of Llanigon was the Rev William Jones Thomas who also served as a magistrate for Breconshire, Herefordshire and Radnorshire. He lived with his wife Annie Elizabeth in a large mansion called Llanthomas (demolished in 1949/50). They had a large family consisting of six sons and five daughters, most of whom are buried in Llanigon churchyard.

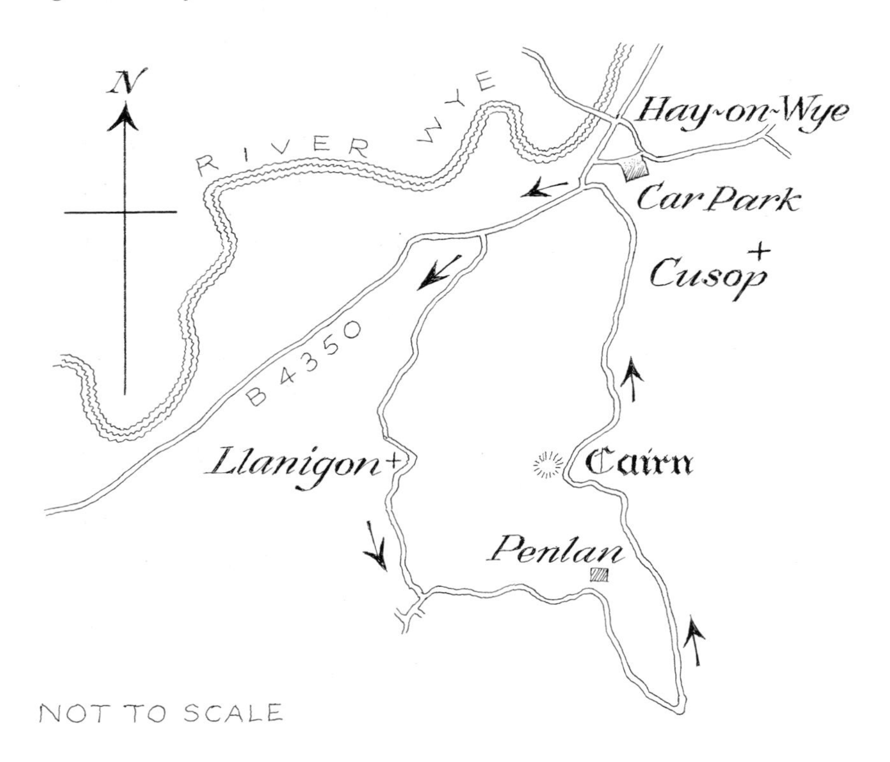

Kilvert was a regular visitor and he fell in love with Fanny, the youngest daughter who he frequently refers to in his *Diary* as Daisy. In September 1871 he set off for Llanthomas to talk to Daisy's father about his feelings for his daughter:

*As I crossed the bridge over the Digedi I wondered with what feelings I should cross the bridge an hour later. The whole family at home came into the drawing room to see me and I was wondering how I could get Mr Thomas away for a private talk, when he said suddenly, 'Come out into the garden.' Daisy came into the room. I thought she coloured and looked conscious. I delivered up to her the basket she had lent me to take the grapes in to Alice Davies and gave her Alice's message of thanks. Then we went out into the garden, her father and I. I said, 'You will be very much surprised but I hope not displeased at what I am going to say to you.' 'What is it?' he said eagerly, 'have you got the living of Glasbury?' 'No, something much nearer to you than that.' 'What is it?' I was silent a minute. I was frightfully nervous. 'I-am-attached-to--one-of-your-daughters,' I said.*

*Just as I made this avowal we came suddenly round a corner upon a gardener cutting a hedge. I feared he had heard my confession, but I was much relieved by being assured that he was deaf. Mr Thomas said I had done quite right in coming to him, though he seemed a great deal taken aback.*

*He said also a great many complimentary things about my 'honourable high-minded conduct,' asked what my prospects were and shook his head over them. He could not allow an engagement under the circumstances, he said, and I must not destroy his daughter's peace of mind by speaking to her or showing her in any way that I was attached to her.*

*The course of true love never does run smooth. What has happened only, makes me long for her more and cling more closely to her, and feel more determined to win her.*

*On this day when I proposed for the girl who will I trust one day be my wife I had only one sovereign in the world, and I owed that.*

Shortly afterwards Kilvert received a letter from Daisy's father, asking him not to pursue the matter any further. One wonders why Kilvert, being so much in love with Daisy, did not return to try his luck again when he had been given the living of St Harmon and also later that of Bredwardine, which certainly made him a more eligible husband.

St Eigon's Church, Llanigon (161/214399) is mainly 15th to 17th century with traces of Norman work. The 14th century porch has an upper storey where the priest once lived and it now houses three bells dated 1670.

'Daisy' Thomas

The grave of 'Daisy' - Frances Eleanor Jane Thomas (1852-1928)

None of the five Thomas girls married ( no doubt due to their father frightening off all the suitors) and 'Daisy' died in 1928 at the age of 76. Her real name was Frances Eleanor Jane Thomas and she is buried near the east end of the churchyard.

From Llanigon Church continue in a southerly direction (right of the lychgate) and after about half-a-mile turn left. Impressive views may be enjoyed to the left as the road ascends. The recently restored manor house on the left is Penllan. In due course the summit of Hay Bluff will be seen ahead and it is interesting to remember that this was one of the routes that Kilvert would have taken on his walks into the Black Mountains. The road dips and climbs, twists and turns and apart from the tarmac surface, little has changed since Kilvert's time.

On reaching a T junction turn left. Ignore the next turning on the left and continue to reach a sharp left hand bend at Pendenallt Farm. From here is an excellent view of Hay-on-Wye and across to the hills above Clyro.

View over Hay-on-Wye from near Pendenallt Farm

As you descend there are open views to the right for a while, but look out for a fingerpost on the left, if you wish to visit the Long Cairn. In front of the fingerpost is a grass track and space for a couple of cars or a minibus. From here it is a walk of about 100 yards to reach the remains of this prehistoric burial chamber.

The Long Cairn is a rectangular chamber of upright stone slabs dating back to Neolithic times. It was excavated in the 1920s.

Return to your vehicle and continue downhill to a T junction. Turn left and within a few minutes you are back in Hay-on-Wye.

# CAR TOUR TO CUSOP AND CLIFFORD

23 miles (37 km)

On leaving the main car park in Hay, turn right to follow the Bredwardine road. After crossing a bridge turn right to follow the road into Cusop Dingle. Take the next turning on the left (signposted St Mary's Church).

Park near the lychgate of **Cusop Church** (GR 241416) which is situated on high ground on the Herefordshire side of the Dulas Brook. This tributary of the Wye rises in the Black Mountains and descends Cusop Dingle marking the boundary between England and Wales.

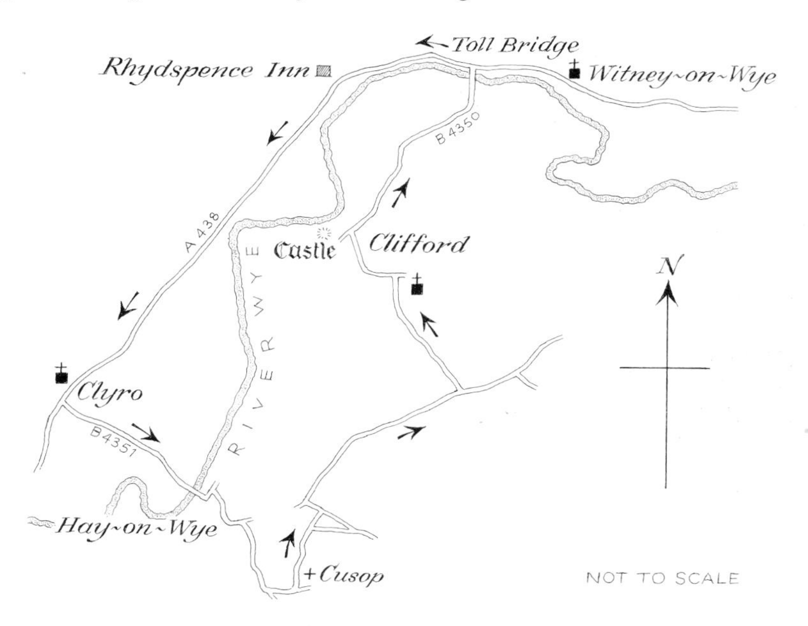


Four ancient yews guard the churchyard and three of them are marked on the Domesday Survey. One of them has a girth of some 30 feet. Beneath one of these remarkable trees is the 'Martyr's Grave', the last resting place of William Seward, a follower of Wesley and George Whitfield, who was killed by a local mob whilst preaching here.

Cusop Church is dedicated to St Mary and is said to have been established by the monks of Llanthony before 1100. It is a simple building with a fine Norman chancel arch while the roof of the nave is 17th century. The font with its trellis pattern is not less than 700 years old. The church was restored in 1857 at a cost of £700.

St Mary's Cusop was restored in 1857

Cusop Castle stood on a mound just beyond the churchyard

Kilvert tells an amusing tale of his friend Pope, the young curate of Cusop, who had an unfortunate experience when the Bishop of Hereford mistook him for a candidate for Confirmation at Whitney Church.

*In Hadley's shop (Hay) I met Dewing who told me of a most extraordinary misfortune that befell Pope the curate of Cusop yesterday at the Whitney Confirmation. He had one candidate Miss Stokes a farmer's daughter and they went together by train. Pope went in a cutaway coat very short, with his dog, and took no gown. The train was very late. He came very late into the church and sat down on a bench with the girl cheek by jowl. When it came to his turn to present his candidate he was told by the Rector (Henry Dew) or someone in authority to explain why he came so late. The Bishop of Hereford (Atlay) has a new fashion of confirming only two persons at a time, kneeling at the rails. The Bishop had marked two young people come in very late and when they came up to the rails he thought from Pope's youthful appearance and from his having no gown that he was a young farmer candidate and brother of the girl. He spoke to them severely and told them to come on and kneel down for they were extremely late. Pope tried to explain that he was a clergyman and that the girl was his candidate but the Bishop was overbearing and imperious and either did not hear or did not attend, seeming to think he was dealing with a refractory ill-conditioned youth. 'I know, I know,' he said. 'Come at once, kneel down, kneel down.' Poor Pope resisted a long time and had a long battle with the Bishop, but at last unhappily he was overborne in the struggle, lost his head, gave way, knelt down and was confirmed there and then, and no one seems to have interfered to save him, though Mr Palmer of Eardisley and others were sitting close by and the whole Church was in a titter. It is a most unfortunate thing and will never be forgotten and it will be unhappily a joke against Pope all his life. The Bishop was told of his mistake afterwards and apologised to Pope, though rather shortly and cavalierly. He said, what was quite true, that Pope ought to have come in his gown. But there was a little fault on all sides for if the Bishop had been a little less hasty, rough and overbearing in his manner things might have been explained, and the bystanding clergy were certainly very much to blame for not stepping forward and preventing such a farce. I fear poor Pope will be very much vexed, hurt and dispirited about it.*

As Curate of Cusop, Pope was in sole charge of the parish of Cusop and thus had greater responsibility than Kilvert. He later moved to Preston-on-Wye and married Miss Hariet Mary Ernle Money-Kyrle

The wedding of Andrew Pope and Hariet Mary Ernle Money-Kyrle of Homme House, Much Marcle., which was attended by Kilvert.

After their honeymoon in Paris, Pope built the vicarage at Preston -on-Wye, decorating it with a plaque bearing his initials and the date of the rebuilding. He even considered pulling down the church and moving it nearer to the village!

In 1880 he took up the living of Diddlesbury near Ludlow and his final position was at Langley Burrell (which by a strange coincidence was the home of Kilvert's parents), where he retired in 1910. He died at Ross-on-Wye in 1924 leaving the impressive sum of about £22,000.

To see the site of Cusop Castle, walk up the lane opposite the lychgate for a short distance to reach a gate on the right. From here you can see the site of the castle in the field (private land). There is no stonework remaining but this was once one of the many border fortresses built in Medieval times.

Return to your vehicle and drive back down the way that you have come. Very shortly turn right, to follow a narrow lane; turn left at the next junction and then shortly right to follow the B4348. Take the next turning on the left. On reaching a T-junction, turn right and shortly park on the right near the entrance to **Clifford Church** (GR 252451).

Clifford Church was built in the 12th century and substantially re-constructed in Victorian times

Inside Clifford Church can be seen this very fine wooden effigy which is believed to represent the founder of Clifford Priory. At the time of the Dissolution it was brought to the church for preservation. It used to be carried around the church in procession on Founder's Day and the holes in the shoulders were no doubt for the poles on which it was supported to be inserted.

This church was substantially rebuilt in Victorian times but it has one item of particular interest inside, a rare oak figure of a priest with his hands clasped on his breast. Considering that it must be at least 600 years old, this carving is beautifully preserved and may represent a one-time Rector of Clifford who officiated here, between 1270 and 1280. It is one of just ninety-six wooden effigies that have survived in Great Britain, and the only other one in Herefordshire is at Much Marcle. The vicar in Kilvert's day was the Rev William Trumper who came from Grosmont in Monmouthshire. His wife, Elizabeth was a native of Llangarron, Herefordshire.

When you come out of the church turn right and follow a grass path which was often used by Kilvert, down to a metal gate and then cross a field to reach a stile in a hedge. Go over the stile and enter the field to take in the view.

In the valley below can be seen Priory Farm, but the grand house called Clifford Priory (built in about 1860) where the home of the Allen family lived was burnt down in the 1930s.

Priory Farm stands on the site of a small cell of Cluniac monks which was founded by Simon Fitzwalter in Henry II's reign. The farm incorporates fragments of the Norman priory and there are also traces of old fishponds.

> *Walked to Clifford Priory across the fields with Crighton and Barton...A crowd in the drawing room drinking claret cup iced and eating enormous strawberries... the usual set that one meets and knows so well. Dews, Thomases, Webbs, Wyatts, Bridges, Oswalds, Trumpers, etc... Everyone about here is so pleasant and friendly that we meet almost like brothers and sisters. Great fun on the lawn, 6 cross games of croquet and balls flying in all directions. High tea at 7.30... After tea we all strolled out into the garden and stood on the high terrace to see the eclipse... It was very strange and solemn... The ladies' light dresses looked ghostly in the dark and at a little distance it was almost impossible to tell which was a lady in a white dress and which was a clump of tall white lilies.*

Clifford Priory, before it was burned down in 1930, was the home of Benjamin Haigh Allen who was a magistrate and deputy Lieutenant of Herefordshire. He was born in Huddersfield and his wife Mary Sophia came from Canterbury. They had two daughters: Mary Lucy and Emily Kate.

*Clifford Priory is certainly one of the nicest most comfortable houses in this part of the country. The evening was exquisite and the party wandered out into the garden promiscuously after dinner under the bright moon which shone alone in the unclouded sky. When the party re-assembled in the drawing room there was music, and meanwhile I had a long talk in the recessed window and moonlight with Helen of Troy. She and her sister were dressed prettily in blue, the most elegant and tasteful dresses I have seen this year. Mrs Allen asked me to a croquet party here next Tuesday, and Mr Allen asked me to luncheon at Oakfield on Monday when the Foresters are coming to his house. He brought me as far as Hay in the rumble of his most antiquated most comfortable old yellow chariot on C springs, very large broad and heavy and able to carry 7 people. We had 6 on board, Mrs Allen, Thomas and Pope inside, I preferred the night air and the tramping of the fast mare. Going up hills we had before us the antiquated figure of the old coachman against the sky and amongst the stars. So we steadily rumbled into Hay....*

Now return to your vehicle and drive back down hill to reach the main road (B4350). Directly opposite will be seen the ruins of **Clifford Castle**. (Not open to the public at the time of writing).

Perched on a grassy knoll above the Wye, Clifford Castle was initially constructed as a motte and bailey by William FitzOsbern, Earl of Hereford and just below it is the ford from which the parish later took its name. The castle is mentioned in Domesday Book and at the time of that great survey (1080) it was in the hands of Ralph de Todeni. With the river on one side and a moat on the other the site was easily defended. This was one of five castle sites which were given to FitzOsborn by the Conqueror and after the 'wild Welsh' had been subjugated it was probably used as a hunting lodge.

Clifford Castle, overlooking the River Wye is in private ownership

About eighty years after the Conquest, the castle passed by marriage to a knight who took the surname of de Clifford and it was the birthplace of Jane de Clifford, who on account of her renowned beauty was called 'Rosa Mundi' - 'Rose of the World'. This fair young maid, daughter of Walter de Clifford became the mistress of Henry II, much to the disgust of Queen Eleanor.

Rosamund spent a great deal of time in Woodstock, near Oxford, and died in 1175 at Godstow Priory, where tradition has it that she was poisoned by Queen Eleanor. On Rosamund's grave an elegiac couplet was carved:

'Hic jacet in tumba Rosa mundi non Rosa munda<br>Non redolet sed olet quae redolere solet.'

When the Clifford family moved to the North of England, their Wye Valley castle was acquired by the Mortimers, who were perhaps the most famous of all the Marcher families.

Turn right along the B4350 and follow it to reach Clifford Toll Bridge which provides a crossing point on the Wye at a current charge of 50p per car. Built in 1797, this is one of the last remaining privately owned toll bridges in Great Britain. By an 18th century Act of Parliament the bridge does not incur rates or taxes.

Whitney Toll Bridge is privately owned and it has been rebuilt a number of times. It has stone abutments with a timber-framed carriageway, timber piers and timber cutwaters. There is a weight limit of 7.5 tonnes and the speed limit is 5 mph.

*We went to Whitney Bridge and Jack, Edward and Walter rowed and punted up with us in two boats to Cabalva. It was very beautiful on the river and a most picturesque sight was two white swans in flight flapping slowly up the beds of the river, snowy against the dark green trees and above the dark grassy stream.*

Georgii III Regis
Anno Dominii 1796
Tolls Vested by Act of Parliament
Twelfth Day of July

| | The Sum of |
|---|---|
| For every horse, mare, gelding, ox, or other beast drawing any carriage...... | 4½d. |
| For every horse, mare, gelding, laden, unladen, and not drawing............. | 2d. |
| For every person or foot passenger.. | 1d. |
| For every score of oxen, cows, or neat cattle........................................ | 10d. |
| –and so in proportion for any greater or less number– | |
| And for every score of calves, hogs, sheep or lambs................ | 5d. |
| –and so in proportion for any greater or less number – | |
| *At a later date, two more tolls were added:* | |
| For every ass drawing any cart....... | 2d. |
| For every dog drawing any cart.... | 2d. |

These tolls are no longer applicable!

Turn left along the A438 which leads back to Clyro and then Hay-on-Wye via the B4351. On the way you may like to stop at the ***Rhydspence Inn,*** which is signposted just off the main road on the right. This attractive building stands within a few yards of the Cwmrafwy Brook, which forms the boundary between Herefordshire and Radnorshire. At one time it was known as the 'last house in England' and served customers as long ago as 1350.

**Rhydspence** was once an important collecting centre for the Welsh drovers, who knew it as 'The Cattle Inn', for it was on the route for cattle and poultry taken 'on the hoof' from Wales to the English markets with some drives going as far as Smithfield in London.

The *Rhydspence Inn* was once frequented by drovers and is situated close to the border of England and Wales

During these rustic times of the late 18th century when the cattle trade was at its height, the tranquillity of this spot must have been greatly disturbed by the shouts and bawdy songs of the Welsh drovers, taking their refreshment here before continuing the drive down to a ford on the Wye.

The big porch-room above the entrance was once known as the Head Drovers' Room and there is a tiny peephole in the left hand wall. A look-out was stationed here to watch for the appearance of the large herds coming down the steep lane descending Brilley Mountain behind the inn. It was customary for the drovers, who were the men in charge, to sleep in the inn while the younger men bedded down near the cattle to feed and guard them.

To cope with the hard surface of roads on the drovers' route, the cattle had to be shod and Rhydspence was an important shoeing centre on the Welsh border. A good smith could shoe as many as sixty or seventy animals a day and his charge at one time was twopence a beast. Even the geese, which were driven in large numbers, had to be shod to cope with the long journey. This was done by compelling the birds to walk through alternate layers of tar and sand which stuck to their feet and provided protection on their arduous march.

When Kilvert passed through Rhydspence at midnight in 1873, he found *the English inn was still ablaze with light and noisy with the songs of revellers, but the Welsh inn was dark and still.* The Welsh inn (the Cabalva Arms) was on the west side of the Cwmrafwr Brook, directly opposite the Rhydspence, and it is now a private house.

Years ago the **Rhydspence** was noted for its excellent cider, and the old horse-operated press and cider mill still stand in the yard outside the inn. They were in use until 1956.

The old horse-operated cider press in the yard outside the *Rhydspence Inn* was used until 1956. At one time nearly every farm in Herefordshire had a cider mill, for this County is among the great cider making areas of the world with orchards of cider apples a familiar sight in the landscape.

> *On the border by the old white and black striped timbered house, the Rhydspence Inn, the weeping willow still drooped like a green shower, and the boundary brook of Cwmrafor came leaping and foaming down the beautiful goats' dingle under the green shadow of the sunlit weeping willows and silver birches swiftly flashing.*

## WALK 6

## *To Bettws Chapel*

(2 ½ miles 4 km)

(Note: This walk involves a fairly steep ascent)

Walk up the road past the *Rhydspence Inn* for a short way to re-enter Wales. On the left is Rhydspence Cottage which was once a public house. Just above it go through a gate near a finger post and head straight up the field. A steady ascent, passing to the right of a lone tree brings you to a gate at the top of the field.

Bear left to pass beneath the power lines to reach a stile, to the left of the poles. Cross a gravel track and go over a stile directly opposite. Continue through the next field to join a rutted track, which curves around beneath a hedge to meet a gate. Evidence of a cobbled surface will be seen, indicating that this was once a route of some importance.

The track leads on through the trees to cross an ancient stone bridge spanning a deep dingle and further on it passes below a semi-derelict cottage, named *Old House*. It was most certainly occupied in Kilvert's time.

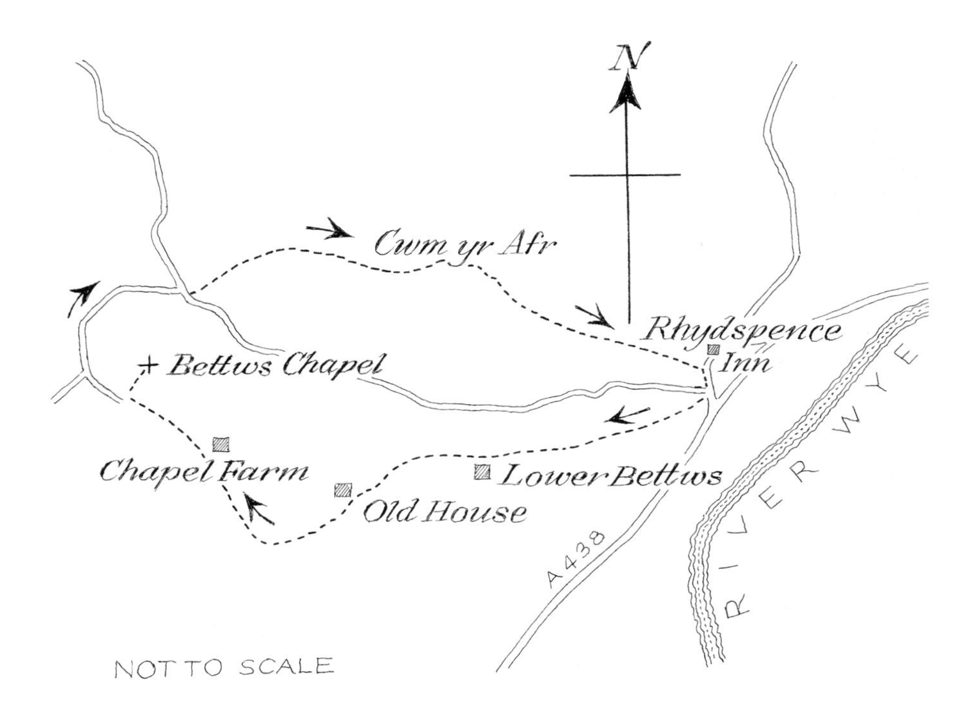

Go through a gate and keep straight on to shortly pass through another gateway. The track now ascends and bends around to the right. On reaching a path junction, keep to the right with the gradient now more gentle. It leads on through a gate and the cobbled surface is well preserved on this section. Pass through two more gates in quick succession, to the left of Chapel Farm.

**Bettws Chapel** comes into view and the lane now has a gravel surface. A small wooden gate on the right gives access to a field through which one walks to reach the Chapel. (The key is kept at a bungalow at the top of this lane).

The Rev Richard Lister Venables and the Rev Francis Kilvert used to take it in turns to conduct Sunday services here, but the chapel that they knew must have looked very different to the one we see today. Bettws Clyro is unique among Radnorshire churches in that it has no dedication, at least none that is known today.

The small and isolated Holy Trinity Chapel Bettws Clyro (GR 228474) is situated in a field high up above Clyro and it served the farms in this corner of the parish. It was completely rebuilt after Kilvert's time in 1878, but the uprights on rood beams of a 14th century screen have been preserved. Two of the roof principals terminate in rudely carved figures and possibly date from the 15th century. Also of interest is the 13th century font bowl which was brought here from Clyro Church.

*In the Chapel field the tall brown and purple grasses wereall in billows like the sea, as the wind coursed over the hill driving one billow after another, sheen and dusk, up against the Chapel wall. And the Chapel in the grass looked like a house founded upon a rock in the midst of a billowy sea.*

A drawing by Kilvert's sister Dora, of the interior of Bettws Chapel in 1865

After visiting the Chapel continue up the lane and turn right to follow a tree shaded road to reach another road junction. Directly opposite go over a stile beside a finger post and gate. Continue straight across a field to a gate in a hedge and then across the next field to a stile in the bottom right corner. Keeping the hedge/fence on your left walk on beside a deep dingle, enjoying fine views towards the Black Mountains.

Cross two stiles in quick succession and keeping the fence on your left go down the next field to a stile. It seems a long descent making you aware of the height that you have climbed on this walk.

Go over another stile and as you descend the last field, the *Rhydspence Inn* comes into sight. Go through a gate and over the last stile to reach the road. Turn left for the *Rhydspence Inn* car park.

## CAR TOUR TO CAPEL-Y-FFIN AND LLANTHONY

25 miles (40 km)

On the 5th April, 1870 Kilvert, Morrell and Bridge (from Pontfaen just outside Hay-on-Wye) went by carriage to Llanigon, then walked past Cilonw Farm and over the Gospel Pass to Capel-y-ffin. We have already visited Llanigon so will now take the direct route from Hay-on-Wye to the Gospel Pass.

A short distance past the Swan Hotel turn left and follow the road to Capel-y-ffin via the mountain pass (1,778 feet) between Hay Bluff and Lord Hereford's Knob.

This is a road to be avoided on summer weekends for it is narrow with few passing places. On weekdays, however, it is generally much quieter and one is not so likely to get caught up in the nightmare of a traffic jam which can sometimes stretch in both directions.

It was not until the mid 1950's that this road was surfaced from Capel-y-ffin to Hay. Old guide books used to issue the adventurous motorist a challenge by providing the tempting information that in dry conditions it was possible to take your Austin Seven beyond Capel-y-ffin and over the pass to Hay-on-Wye. But it was not a journey for the feint hearted.

Many people who come to this narrow gap between Twmpa and Hay Bluff must wonder how it was given the name Bwlch yr Efengyl, which means 'Pass of the Evangelist'. Well, according to legend, St Peter once passed this way with his brother Paul on their mission into Wales to evangelise the heathen Silures. It is said that as a result this wild spot became known as 'The Pass of the Evangelist', or as it is called today the Gospel Pass. However neither saint ever set foot in Britain, so the name must have a much different origin.

The view from here is particularly fine and it has even been claimed that on a clear day Cadair Idris in Snowdonia can be seen 60 miles away. In good visibility one may certainly make out Plynlimmon where the Wye and Severn have their source. In the middle distance you may see the sun shining on the mass of Mynydd Epynt and to the west the Brecon Beacons standing proud with their distinctive table-like summits. Directly ahead are the rounded tops of the Radnor hills while in the valley below, the River Wye curves in its great loop from Builth to Whitney.

On the west side of the pass is the easily ascended Twmpa, while to the east is the rim of Ffynnon y parc leading to the summit of Pen y Beacon or Hay Bluff which is the most northerly point of the Black Mountains. It is also a popular launching point for hang gliding and para-gliding enthusiasts who make good use of the air currents to soar and float gently down to the flat Hay common directly below.

*It always interests me to think that probably in their walks from Llyswen to Llanthony William and Dora Wordsworth crossed the mountain by this pass. The level searching sunlight struck out every scar and water course on the broad bare mountain side. There was no sound except the shepherds calling to their dogs about the hills.*

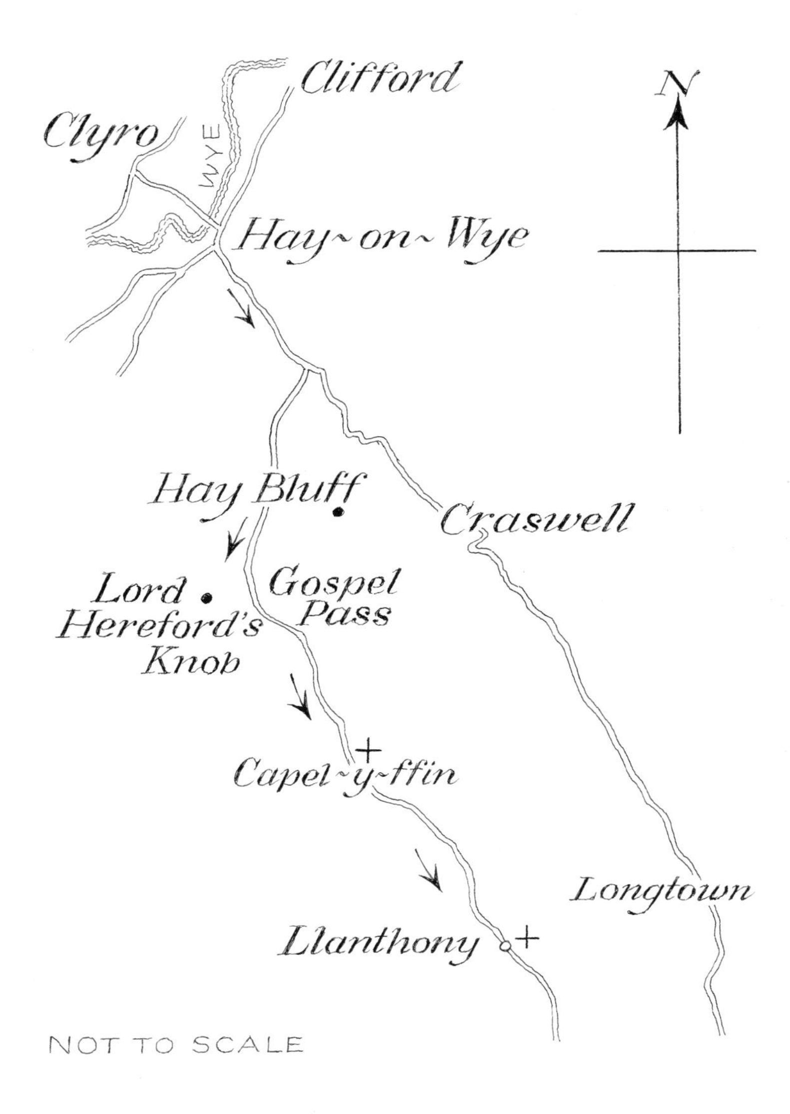

Follow the road down to reach the tiny hamlet of **Capel-y-ffin** (GR 255315) which nestles in these hills at an altitude of 1,050 feet above sea level. It must surely be the most holy hamlet imaginable for there are no less than three religious establishments to be found here. Two chapels are situated in the valley beside the Honddu while on the hillside above is the Victorian monastery established by Father Ignatius.

This little church at Capel-y-ffin reminded Kilvert of an owl

The name Capel-y-ffin means 'Chapel-of-the-boundary'. This stems from the fact that it is situated at the boundary of the old counties of Monmouthshire, Breconshire and Herefordshire. It is also the meeting place of three dioceses: Hereford, St. David and Llandaff.

Set in a circle of yews the little whitewashed church dedicated to St Mary was built in 1762, replacing one established here in the 15th century. The south porch was added in 1817. It is a picturesque building, with a sandstone tiled roof and a small wooden bell turret which sits astride the roof and leans at a drunken angle.

When Kilvert came here in 1870 he described the church in his diary as being *short, stout and boxy...the quiet peaceful chapel graveyard shaded by the seven great solemn yews.* He also commented that the building reminded him of an owl which indeed it certainly resembles, when approached along the pathway leading from the gate.

The graveyard is well worth inspecting for it contains a fascinating assortment of memorial stones. Some of them were carved by Eric Gill, the famous artist and sculptor, who came to live at Capel-y-ffin monastery in 1924. One inscription invites us to remember a local fellow who was employed as Eric Gill's handyman :

'Remember Charlie Stones - Carpenter, died 1935 - R.I.P'

Another particularly touching epitaph in this graveyard commemorates little Noah Watkins, aged eight:

'In memory of Noah, ye son of Noah Watkins,
who died aged 8 years in 1738.This child said
he would not take A hundred pounds for
Breaking the sabbath, but keep it holy.'

The dimensions of the church are 28 feet by 18 feet, and it is said to be able to accommodate 40 worshippers, most of whom would have to sit in the gallery which runs along two sides of the building. This gallery, nearly doubles the seating capacity and the memorials which one would expect to find on the inner walls have had to be fixed to the outside of the building.

The pulpit is dated 1780 and the font appears to be supported by an inverted bowl which may be an older font. There are two bells, one dated 1716, the other, claimed to be pre-Reformation, was the gift of Father Ignatius.

On the other side of the river is the equally small Baptist Chapel which was built in 1762 when David and William Prosser gave a piece of land on which it could be built. Just below the footbridge leading to the chapel is a pool where baptisms once took place. Inside the chapel, three steps on each side lead to the pulpit and here too is a gallery which dominates the interior.

*I had not seen Capel y Ffin for 4 years but I remembered the place perfectly, the old chapel short stout and boxy with its little bell turret (the whole building reminded one of an owl), the quiet peaceful chapel yard shaded by the seven great solemn yews, the chapel house, a farm house over the way, and the Great Honddu brook crossing the road and crossed in turn by the stone foot bridge. Before the chapel house door by the brookside a buxom comely wholesome girl with fair hair, rosey face, blue yes, and fair skin stood washing at a tub in the sunshine, up to the elbows of her round white lusty arms in soapsuds. We asked her how far it was to the place where the monks were building their monastery. 'Oh,' she said, smiling kindly and stopping her washing for a moment to direct us. 'Oh, none just. Please to go over the brook and up the lane.' Two tramps were lounging against the bridge lighting their pipes and said to each other when we had passed, 'They are only going to see the monks'.*

Two of the Capel-y-ffin monks doing a spot of fishing in the Honddu

*A few minutes walk up a lane now dry but which is a watercourse in winter, and looking through the hedge we exclaimed, 'There they are'. Two black figures were working in a sloping patch of ground laid out as a garden, one digging and the other wheeling earth to him in a barrow. They were dressed in long black habits girt round the waist with scourge cords knotted at the ends and dangling almost to the ground. The black hoods or cowls were drawn over their heads leaving their faces bare, and their naked feet were thrust into sandals with which they went slip slop along as with slippers down at heel. Father Philip was digging. Brother Serene or Cyrene was wheeling earth to him from a heap thrown out of the excavation dug for the foundations of the monastery. He seemed very much oppressed by his heavy black dress, for the sun was hot and he stopped when he had wheeled his empty barrow back to the heap and stood to rest and wipe his streaming brow. They both seemed studiously unconscious of our presence, but I saw Brother Serene glancing furtively at us from under his cowl when he thought he was under cover of the heap of earth. We at first thought of speaking to them but decided not to afterwards, fearing they might think our trespassing an intrusion on their privacy, uncourteous and rude. We spoke to the masons of whom there were two working on the foundations. They spoke with great respect and some awe of the monks and did not seem the least inclined to laugh at them. They answered all our questions too very civilly. We saw the foundation stone which Father Ignatius came down to lay three weeks ago. Then he returned to London and at present there are only these two monks in residence. They have one servant a young man who was also wheeling earth. They lodge at a farmhouse close by and live a good deal on milk. They allow no woman to come near them and do their own washing. Probably however there is little of that to do. They may wear linen but don't show any and perhaps they did not take off their habits when at work because they had nothing under. They looked very much like old women at work in the garden. It does seem very odd at this stage of the world in the latter part of the 19th century to see monks gravely wearing such dresses and at work in them in broad day. One could not help thinking how much more sensible and really religious was the dress and occupation of the masons and of the hearty healthy girl washing at the Chapel House, living naturally in the world and taking their share of its work, cares and pleasures, than the morbid unnatural life of these monks going back into the errors of the dark ages and shutting themselves from the world to pray for the world. 'Laborare est Orare.' The masons had raised the foundation walls to the level of the ground and believed the house would be built by the end of May, which I doubt. The monks as usual had chosen a pretty and pleasant place on a fine slope at the foot of the mountain where there was good soil and plenty of water, a trout stream and sand for mortar. The house which seemed from the ground plan, as far as we could make it out, to be a long shallow building will look S.E. down the valley towards Llanthony Abbey. The monks have bought 32 acres. It is said they have collected £50,000 which may probably be divided by 10. Very few people came to the ceremony of laying the foundation stone.*

The monastery of Father Ignatius at Capel-y-ffin

On leaving Capel-y-ffin, drive down the valley for about 4 miles to reach a turning on the left which leads up to a car park at **Llanthony Priory**. Kilvert came here on foot:

*We crossed a field and the fold of a farmhouse, scrambled down a stony lane and struck the main road again. About a mile above Llanthony we descried the Abbey ruins, the dim grey pile of building in the vale below standing by the little river side among its brilliant green meadow. What was our horror on entering the enclosure to see two tourists with staves and shoulder belts all complete postured among the ruins in an attitude of admiration, one of them of course discoursing learnedly to his gaping companion and pointing out objects of interest with his stick. If there is one thing more hateful than another it is being told what to admire and having objects pointed out to one with a stick. Of all noxious animals too the most noxious is a tourist. And of all tourists the most vulgar, illbred, offensive and loathsome is the British tourist. No wonder dogs fly at them and consider them vermin to be exterminated. The most offensive part of their conduct however was that they arrived before us and already ordered their dinner, so we had to wait till they had done, solacing ourselves with the 'Hereford Times' and the Visitors' Book from which to the great and just indignation of the landlord some of the British tourists had cut out and stolen half a year of entries from October 1865 to May 1866, including my last entry.*

*Meanwhile we bought photographs of the Abbey and little books about Llanthony and the Black Mountains, and I strolled alone about the ruins and up the beautiful nave where the row of fair grey pointed arches rises from the close green turf, and under the great central tower where the high altar used to stand. A rude cross legged table stood on the turf of the Choir beneath which probably lie Hugh and William de Laci.*

*We were hungry and our ham and eggs fried and served in a pretty upper room were very acceptable. We had also good bread cheese and butter and fair beer for which we paid 2/- each.*

The *Abbey Hotel* at Llanthony Priory was known as the *Travellers' Rest* in Kilvert's time

*We could not have had a more beautiful day for our excursion. Under the cloudless blue and glorious sunshine the Abbey looked happy and peaceful like a man in calm happy beautiful old age. And the tender blue haze that veiled the hills made the happy valley look like fairyland.*

*Morell and I arrived at Clyro 7.50 and dined together comfortably at Cae Mawr sitting up talking afterwards till past twelve. We were rather tired with our 25 miles walk, but not extraordinarily so.*

St David is said to have established a small mud and wattle shrine here some fourteen centuries ago. He lived in this once remote valley in peace and meditation for a few years and his simple building became known as Llandewi nant Honddu (the Church of St David on the brook of the black water), a name which was later corrupted by the Normans into Llanthoni and this in due course became Llanthony.

Towards the end of the reign of William II, a Norman retainer of the Earl of Hereford named William de Lacy rode into this valley in search of game. He became separated from his hunting companions and following the river, came to the ruined hermitage of St David, where he stopped for a rest. Until then William had led an evil life; but he was deeply affected by this holy place, and so strong were his convictions that he decided to remain here in sanctity and prayer for the rest of his life. The historian Dugdale commented that:

> *'William laid aside his belt and girded himself with a rope; instead of fine linen, he covered himself with haircloth; and instead of his soldier's robe he loaded himself with weighty irons. The suit of armour, which before defended him from the darts of his enemies, he still wore as a garment to harden himself against the soft temptations of his old enemy, Satan; that as the outward man was afflicted by austerity, the inner man might be secured for the service of God. That his zeal might not cool, he thus crucified himself, and continued this hard armour on his body until it was worn out with rust and age.'*

After a number of years of solitary living, William was visited in 1103 by Ernisius, a chaplain to the Court of Queen Matilda, who was so impressed by William's piety that he stayed as partner and companion. The Earl of Hereford offered donations so that a church of strength and dignity might be built, but the now pious William, fearing any such affluence, refused the gift. The two men decided to become members of the strict order of St Augustine, which they considered 'free of the falsities and hypocrisy of other brotherhoods.'

William's strict scruples were eventually overcome, and, against his will, he accepted money to build a more permanent building. The present one was begun in 1108 and it was dedicated five years later by Urban, Bishop of Llandaff and Reynelm, Bishop of Hereford.

This building became the hospitium or infirmary hall and chapel of the Priory and this is borne out by the two doorways at the east end of the nave and the length of its chancel, uncommon for the period.

The ruined nave at Llanthony Priory

It is interesting that the church is sited so that its axis is aligned with the sun as it rises over Hatterrall Hill on St David's Day, March 1st. Likewise the ruined church of the nearby priory (dedicated to St John the Baptist) is orientated for the Baptist's Day, June 24th.

After the Dissolution of the Monasteries the old church became the Parish church and the chancel may be the actual cell built by the first hermit, William de Lacy and Ernisius, at the beginning of the 12th century on the site of the former chapel of St David.

This is in fact confirmed by Giraldus Cambrensis, who writing in 1188, just 80 years after the consecration of the church comments that it stands 'on the very spot where the humble chapel of St David had formerly stood, decorated with only ivy and moss.'

Up to 1844 the church was in the ancient Diocese of St Davids in Pembrokeshire. It then became part of the Diocese of Llandaff and in 1921 it was transferred to the Diocese of Monmouth.

On receiving endowments from Hugh de Lacy, William and Ernisius founded a monastery for Black canons of the Order of St Augustine to which were admitted forty monks. Robert de Behune succeeded Ernisius as prior and under his direction the present structure of the Priory was completed.

Soon after it was built, the Priory gave shelter to another illustrious convert, Walter de Gloucester, Earl of Hereford, Keeper of Grosmont Castle and hereditary Constable of England. He had decided to dispose of his many possessions, including the lordship of Abergavenny - to his son Milo and end his days as an Austin canon at Llanthony.

During the civil war between Stephen and Matilda the Priory was subjected to an incident which did much to bring about its premature dissolution. Driven through the valley by his relentless enemies, a Welsh chieftain and his followers sought the right of protective sanctuary within the Priory walls. With the Welshmen's enemies camped outside the walls, determined to capture them the moment they came out, the building was besieged. Provisions could not be brought into the Priory, and it was so difficult to house the refugees, the brothers could not carry out their many religious offices.

After suffering further pillage and oppression the brothers were so distressed that they appealed to the Bishop of Hereford for assistance. At first they were given a temporary home at Hereford, and later they were granted land to build a daughter church on the banks of the Severn near Gloucester. So, in 1136, within thirty years of building the mother church at Llanthony, they began to build a new priory which was called by the same name.

Llanthony Priory is beautifully situated in the heart of the Vale of Ewyas

At Gloucester the monks enjoyed the material benefits of noble and royal patronage, and so were reluctant to return to their former home among the mountains.

The new 'Llanthony' prospered, but the faithful who remained at the mother church were now poor and forgotten. If Llanthony Prima was remembered, it was only as a place of penance where offending brothers were sent for their sins.

A licence issued by King Edward IV united the Black Mountain priory of Llanthony, and the priory of Llanthony near Gloucester. This meant that all the valuable land and possessions of the first Priory were transferred to the second one at Gloucester. The common seal of Llanthony Priory was attached to this licence which was in the Chapter House, Westminster, and this seal was later used by the priory of Llanthony near Gloucester.

The estate was bought from the Harley family in 1799 by Col. Mark Wood, MP of Gratton, Surrey. But he cared little for the medieval remains and the east front collapsed shortly before1803. Colonel Wood built a house for use as a shooting lodge into the ruins, utilising the south-west tower, to which he added a roof and Gothic windows. The shooting lodge has survived as the Abbey Hotel.

In 1808 Wood sold the estate for £20,000 to the poet Walter Savage Landor who had grandoise dreams of settling in the Vale of Ewyas as a country squire. He fully intended to restore the magnificent centre-nave of the priory and had many stones taken down and numbered, but they were never replaced and only served to add to the ruined state of the building.

Some distance above the priory, he built a new house called Y Siarpal ('The Sharple') but due to local problems it was never completed. All that remains now is a substantial stable building half hidden in the trees and part of the shell of the intended mansion.

In the Priory's chancel is part of a tomb incised with a Crusader's Cross and part of a foot with a spurred heel. This ancient slab is said to be a fragment of the sepulchre of the noble monk Walter de Gloucester.

Later that year on 2nd September Kilvert returned to Capel-y-Fffin:-

> *At 10.45 started across the fields to Capel y Ffin. I came in sight of the little Capel y Ffin squatting like a stout grey owl among its seven great black yews. I hastened on, and in front of Capel House farm there was the sunny fair haired girl washing at a tub as usual by the brookside, the girl with the blue eyes, not the blue of the sky, but the blue of the sea. 'Is Father Ignatius here?' I asked. 'Yes. at least he was here this morning.' I asked a mason at work upon the building if Father Ignatius was there. 'There he is with his brother,' said the mason. A black robed and cowled monk was walking fast along the bottom of the field towards a barn with Clavering Lyne. Clavering came up to me, but the monk walked quickly on without looking round. Clavering took me to his father and mother, who were sitting on a garden seat under a tree in a pretty little dingle. They had just arrived unexpectedly from Pontrilas having driven up the valley as I came down. It was curious, our meeting thus as it were by chance.*

Father Ignatius (1837-1908)

*Mr and Mrs Lyne came out of their dingle and Mrs Lyne brought up Father Ignatius and introduced us. He struck me as being a man of gentle simple kind manners, excitable, and entirely possessed by one idea. He always spoke to his father and mother as 'Papa' and 'Mamma' and called me 'Father'. I could not persuade him that my name was not Venables. His head and brow are very fine, the forehead beautifully rounded and highly imaginative. The face is a very saintly one and the eyes extremely beautiful, earnest and expressive, a dark soft brown. When excited they seem absolutely to flame. He wears the Greek or early British tonsure all round the temples, leaving the hair of the crown untouched. His manner gives you the impression of great earnestness and single mindedness. The voice and manner are very like Clavering's and it was with difficulty that I could tell which of the two was speaking if I did not see them. Father Ignatius wore the black Benedictine habit with the two loose wings or pieces falling in front and behind, two violet tassels behind, the knotted scourge girdle, a silver cross on the breast, and a brazen or golden cross hanging from the rosary of black beads under the left arm.*

*We walked round the place and then climbed the steep bank above and looked down upon the building. Mrs Lyne gathered some whinberries and gave them to us to eat. They were very nice. They grew along the ground on tiny bushes among a very small delicately twisted pink heath. We saw the monks and novices below issuing from a barn where they had engaged for an hour or so in an 'examination of conscience'. One of the monks was gazing at us. He had conceived an irrepressible desire to see Mrs Lyne again. He did not wish to intrude upon her approach or address her. He simply wanted to see her at a respectful distance and admire her at far off. Mr Lyne said the monk was a man of few and simple wants, content with a little and thankful for small mercies. Beacause the monk had said if he could see Mrs Lyne he would be perfectly happy.*

*Mrs Lyne not having much faith in the larder or resources of the monastery, especially on a Friday, had wisely taken the precaution of bringing with her an honest leg of mutton and two bottles of wine. The monasterial garden provided potatoes and French beans, very good, and we had luncheon under the tree in the dingle, waited on by the novices also cowled and robed in black like the monks. They addressed Father Ignatius as 'dear Father' whenever they spoke to him and bent the knee whenever they approached or passed him.*

*Whist we were at luncheon we heard voices close to us proceeding from the bottom of a deep watercourse or lane on the other side of the hedge. Then a man looked over the hedge and asked his way to Capel y Ffin. Father Ignatius had been sitting talking freely and at ease with his head uncovered, and his cowl lying back on his shoulders. But directly he heard the strange voices and saw the strange face peering over the hedge he dashed the cowl over his head and face and bolted up the bank among the shrubs like a rabbit. I never saw a man so quick on his legs or so sudden in movement. He was gone like a flash of lightning. He has been much intruded on and persecuted and dreads seeing strangers about the place. Last night some men came from Llanthony Abbey and rang the monastery bells violently and were very rude and insolent. However he treated them kindly and they apologised for their conduct and went away conquered.*

*After luncheon we went up to the monastery again and Mr and Mrs Lyne, Clavering and I each laid a stone in the wall. We had to go up a ladder on to the scaffolding and hoarding. Each of us 'walled' our stone for the benefit of the masons. I laid a stone at the particular request of Father Ignatius. The building that the masons are at work on now is the west cloister which is to be fitted up temporarily for the accommodation of the monks. This work was begun in March and ought to be finished long ago. But there was no one to look after the workmen and they did as much or little as they pleased. Father Ignatius thinks that everyone is as good as himself and is perfectly unworldly, innocent and unsuspicious. He gave the contractor £500 at first, took no receipt from him. And so on. The consequence is that he has been imposed upon, cheated and robbed right and left. Father Ignatius took us into the Oratory, a tiny square room in the*

*Cloister, fitted with a lace and silk-covered altar upon which stands a super altar or Tabernacle in which he informed us in a low awestruck voice was 'the Blessed Sacrament'. There was a couch in the room on which he sleeps. The altar lace came from France, and was very expensive. There was a crucifix above the altar. It came from Spain and had been broken, but it was a beautiful figure. Father Ignatius said that once when he was praying Gerald Moultrie who was present saw the crucifix roll its eyes, then turn its head and look at Father Ignatius. Father Ignatius confessed that neither he nor any of the monks had ever seen the crucifix move. He did not know what to think about it, but he could not help believing that Moultrie saw what he declared he saw. He says that Moultrie is not at all an excitable imaginative man. As he was talking about this in a low eager whisper, he looked strange and wild and his eyes were starting and blazing. He apologised for Mr Lyne's not kneeling at the altar by saying that his father did not believe in the Real Presence. He knelt for a moment at the side of the altar.*

*Mr Lyne was anxious to be going as they had ten miles to drive down a bad road to Pontrilas. So they got their dog-cart. Clavering drove and we parted in the lane. They drove off and I remained in the lane talking to Father Ignatius. I had a good deal of conversation with him then and at luncheon time. He told me that Lord Bute came up to see him and the monastery a few days ago, and to make enquiries. He greatly hopes Lord Bute may help him and send him money. The Order of St Benedict, Father Ignatius says, is now worth about £60. The monks are supported entirely by his preaching. He makes £1000 a year. He gets on much better with the Low Church than with the High Church people he says, best of all with the Dissenters who consider and call him a second Wesley. He allows that a man must be of a very rare and peculiar temperament to become and remain a monk. A monk he says must either be a philosopher or a 'holy fool'. He also allows that monkery has a strong tendency to drive people mad. Out of 50 novices he could only reckon on making 3 monks. The rest would probably be failures. One in seven was a large percentage.*

Kilvert describes Father Ignatius as having *a saintly face and eyes extremely beautiful and expressive.*

*One of the novices was a fine noble looking boy, a gentleman's son, with a sweet open face and fair clustering curly hair. He had been sent to the new monastery by his parents to learn to be a monk. The boy seemed to be devoted to Father Ignatius and came running up with a basket of mushrooms he had just bought to show them to the Father. His cowl was thrown back and his fair young head, bright face and sunny hair made a striking contrast with his black robe. 'Yes dear Father. No dear Father.' And off he went in high delight with his mushrooms and the approval of the Father, as happy as a king and much happier. Poor child. I wonder if he will ever become a monk. I hope he is reserved for a better fate. He shook hands with us all before he went off to the barn. His hand was as small, soft and white as a girl's. They called him 'Manny'. Another of the novices, of lower rank in life, one who waited on us at luncheon, had a peculiarly sweet and beautiful face. He is called Brother Placidus.*

*I stood in the lane near the Honddu bridge for some time talking with Father Ignatius. I asked him if he would not find an ordinary dress more convenient and practical and less open to insult and objection. But he scouted the idea of abandoning his distinctive monastic dress. He said he had once given it up for a few days, but he felt like a deserter and traitor till he took to the habit again. Then he again became happy. The Bishop of Gloucester and Bristol, he said, had suggested the same thing, but he turned the tables on the Bishop by asking him why he did not discard his own foolish and meaningless dress, far more irrational than the Benedictine habit, every part of which has its meaning. The Bishop laughed and said there was a good deal in what Father Ignatius said. He thinks the Bishops are coming round to his side. We shook hands and departed. 'Goodbye, Father,' he said with an earnest kindly look, 'and thank you for your good wish. You must come and see us again when we have our guest house ready.' When we parted a little way and our roads had diverged he called out through the half screen of a hazel hedge, 'Father! Will you remember us the next time you celebrate the Holy Communion?' 'Yes,' I replied, 'I will.'*

**Father Ignatius (1837-1908)**

Joseph Leycester Lyne, who at the age of twenty-five adopted the name of 'Father Ignatius,' was born in the Parish of All Hallows, Barking in 1837, but the last thirty-nine years of his life were spent in Monmouthshire.

In 1847 Lyne entered St Paul's School, but in 1852, after suffering corporal punishment for a breech of discipline, he was removed, and his education was completed at private schools at Spalding and Worcester. He had early developed advanced views on sacramental doctrine, and an acquaintance with Bishop Eden procured his admission to Trinity College, Glen Almond.

There he studied theology from 1856 to 1858 and impressed the Warden by his earnest piety. In 1860 he became curate at St Mary's, Plymouth, and soon started a guild for men and boys with himself as Superior, and projected a community house on a monastic pattern, when illness interrupted his activities.

At Bruges, where he went to recruit, he studied the rule of the Benedictine Order. On his return in 1861 he became curate at St George's-in-the-East, London. The following year Lyne began calling himself 'Father Ignatius,' and issued a pamphlet in favour of the revival of monasticism in the Church of England. This publication excited vehement controversy. Lyne then formed a community at Ipswich which was frequently menaced by Protestant violence. From 1866 to 1868 he preached regularly at St Bartholomew's, Moor-lane, and other City churches. But his conduct was so extravagant that he was suspended by Dr A. C. Tait, Bishop of London.

In 1869 Lyne purchased land in Monmouthshire and built Llanthony Abbey, just four miles from the ruins of twelfth century Llanthony Priory. The cost of the buildings was defrayed by friends and the pecuniary returns of Lyne's mission preaching. Accounts of miracles and supernatural visitations enhanced the local prestige of the monastery, of which 'Father Ignatius' constituted himself abbot. But the life of the community never ran smoothly. Few joined the order; in many cases those who joined soon departed. His difficulties were also increased by family quarrels.

His father, who had persistently opposed his son's extreme Anglican practices, repudiated him altogether and publicly denounced his conduct and doctrines. 'Father Ignatius' combined the profession of a cloistered monk with the activities of a wandering friar. When the churches were closed to him, he preached in lecture halls and theatres, and impressed the public everywhere with his eloquence.

Father Ignatius was made a bard of the Gorsedd and assumed the name of Dewi Honddu. When the National Eisteddfod of Wales was held at Brecon in 1889, he spoke at one of the meetings. In his speech he declared his belief that the Welsh Church owed no allegiance to any other. It should, he said, be completely independent of the Church of England and the Church of Rome, having sprung directly from the preaching of the early apostles. He implored his audience to respect their native land and to see that their children were taught the Welsh language.

In 1890-1 he made a missionary tour through Canada and the United States and was cordially invited to preach in the churches of all denominations. He died in October, 1908, and was buried at Llanthony Abbey, Capel-y-ffin.

His tomb bears a Latin inscription which translates: *'Here lies Ignatius of Jesus, O.S.B., Founder of this house and first Abbot, R. I. P. Died 16th October, 1908.'* The Abbey was left to his remaining monks, subject to the right of an adopted son, William Leycester Lyne. In April 1911, it passed into the hands of the Anglo Benedictine community of Caldey, but today is in private ownership.

# CAR TOUR TO THE GOLDEN VALLEY

16 ¾ miles (27 km)

*William and I walked up to the top of Moccas Park, whence we had a glorious view of the Golden Valley shining in the evening sunlight with the white houses of Dorstone scattered about the green hillsides 'like a handful of pearls in a cup of emerald' and the noble spire of Peterchurch rising from out of the heart of the beautiful rich valley which was closed below by the Sugar Loaf and the Skyrrid blue above Abergavenny.*

Rev Francis Kilvert

From the main car park in Hay-on-Wye, follow the Bredwardine road (B4348) for about 1 mile and then turn right (signposted Michaelchurch and Longtown). This quiet country road climbs steadily to a junction.

Turn left here (signposted Dorstone) to follow the road down, keeping straight on at the next junction. The road climbs, twists and turns, then descends. Bear left at a junction (signposted **Dorstone**) to enter the Golden Valley which is so-named because of a misunderstanding by the Normans who translated 'dwr', the Welsh word for water (refering to the river) as 'd'or', the French for Gold. On reaching the B4348 turn first right for 'Dorstone and the Pandy Inn'. There is a large car park in the village by the Dorstone Stores and Post Office.

All that remains of Dorstone Castle is an earthen circular mound about 20 feet high and 90 feet in diameter, surrounded by a dry moat.

# Car Tour – To the Golden Valley

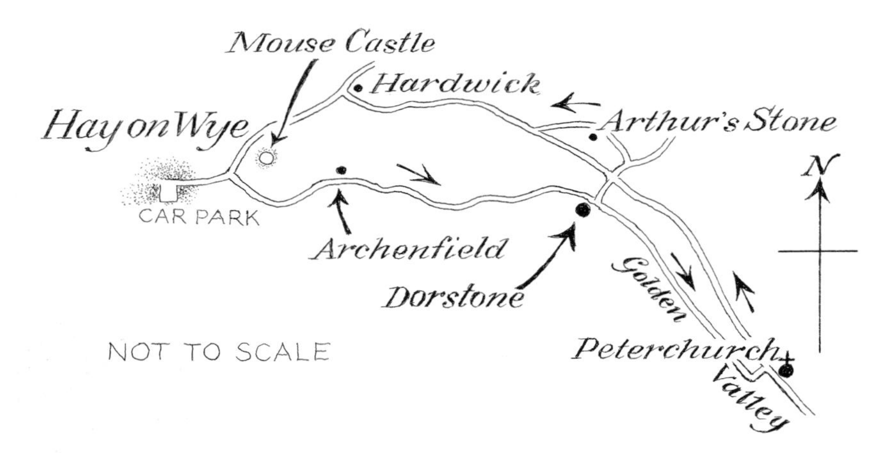

The old village cross in Dorstone is an octagonal shaft set in a base with chamfered angles. On top of the shaft is a metal sundial dated 1812.

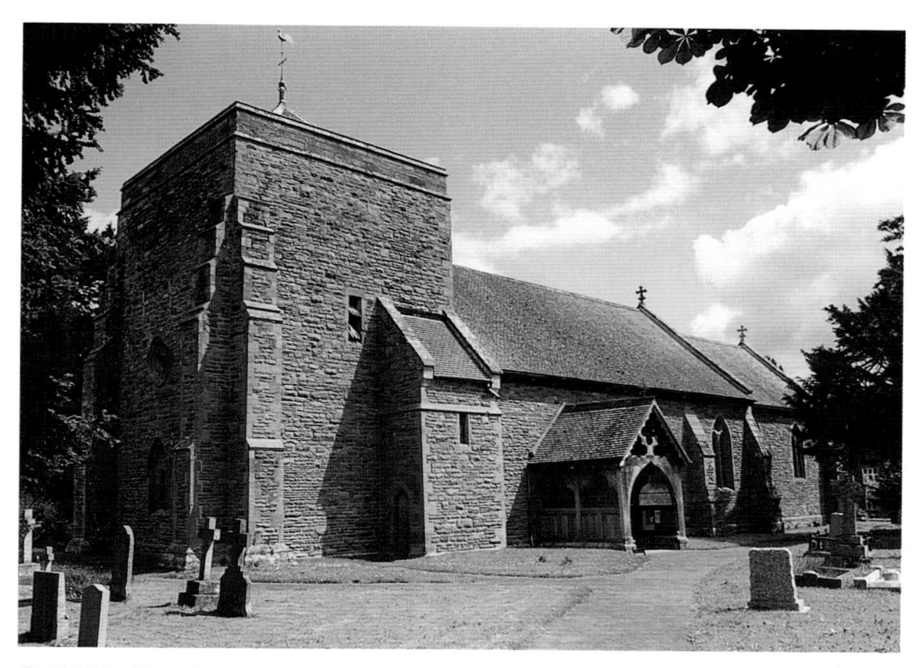

St Faith's Church at Dorstone has a small chantry chapel on the north side of the church which is supposed to have been erected by Richard de Brito, one of the murderers of Thomas à Becket. It was demolished in the course of alterations and a stone in the shape of a window sill was then discovered to bear an inscription: 'Han Capellam ex vodad Mariam Virginem Ricardus de Brito dedicavit.' This stone was subsequently lost.

After looking around Dorstone continue along the road to shortly turn right (signposted Snodhill). On reaching a crossroads turn left (signposted Peterchurch). Look out for a wide grass verge on the left, which provides a convenient parking spot. A walk of about 50 yards will bring you to a wooden gate, giving access to a path leading up to the ruins of **Snodhill Castle**.

The path leads up a grass covered slope and then threads its way around brambles and bushes to the foot of the mound on which the scanty remains of the castle stand. This romantic ruin has probably changed very little since Kilvert's time. The first historical reference to Snodhill occurs in Domesday Book, where it is set down as a possession of Hugh de L'Aisne, who was a comrade of William the Conqueror. One of the famous Chandos family successfully held the castle against Owain Glyndwr but in the following century when Thomas Leland paid a visit to Snodhill, he found it 'somewhat in ruines'.

In later years Elizabeth I granted the manor to Robert Dudley, Earl of Leicester, but he ungratefully sold it within four months. Eventually Snodhill Castle was dismantled to provide materials for building Snodhill Court at the foot of the hill. This was built during the Civil War and the year of the Great Plague is written on a dormer gable.

> *Today we went for a picnic to Snodhill Castle in the Golden Valley...The first thing of course was to scale the Castle Mound and climb up the ruins of the Keep as far as might be. It was fearfully slippery and the ladies gallantly sprawled and struggled up and slithered down again.*
>
> *There was plenty of meat and drink, the usual things, cold chicken, ham and tongue, pies of different sorts, salads, jam and gooseberry tarts, bread and cheese. Splendid strawberries from Clifford Priory brought by the Haigh Allens. Cups of various kinds went round, claret and hock, champagne, cider and sherry, and people sprawled about in all attitudes and made a great noise. Henry Dew was the life of the party and kept the table in a roar. After luncheon the gentlemen entrenched themselves upon a fragment of the Castle wall to smoke and talk local news and politics and the ladies wandered away by themselves.*

The scanty remains of Snodhill Castle, near Dorstone

*At last we all met upon the mound where Mary Bevan and someone else had been trying to sketch the Keep, and sat in a great circle whilst the remains of the cup, wine and soda water were handed round. Then we broke up, the roll of the carriages was heard coming through the lanes below and everyone seized upon something to carry down the steep slippery grass slopes.*

Afterwards the party drove to the Rectory at Dorstone, a mile or so north-east of Snodhill. Here they dined, then stripped the carpet in the drawing room and had an impromptu dance.

Dorstone Rectory is situated about a mile north-east of Snodhill at the head of the Golden Valley.

*At the Rectory we strolled about the garden. Dinner was announced, quite unnecessarily as far as I was concerned, for I wanted nothing. The room too was steaming hot. After dinner the carpet was taken up in the drawing-room and there was a dance on the slippery dark oak floor which was sadly scratched and scored by the nailed boots of the gentlemen and some of the ladies. Tom Powell slipped and fell. Tom Brown, dancing a waltz with his nephew Arthur Oswald, came down with a crash that shook the house and was immediately seized head and heels by Henry Dew and Mr Allen and carried about the room. We danced the Lancers, and finished with Jim Rufen but it was almost too hot. Then the carriages were ordered and we came away.*

*The drive home in the cool of the evening was almost the pleasantest part of the day. The light was so strong that we could hardly believe it was ten o' clock. The longest day, and the strong light glow in the North showed that the Midsummer sun was only just travelling along below the horizon, ready to show again in five hours. Passing by Hawkswood and the ghost-haunted pool we told ghost stories until Mrs Oswald was almost frightened out of the carriage.*

Return to your vehicle, enjoying the views into this beautiful valley. Then continue along the road to turn right at a T-junction and follow a narrow lane leading to **Peterchurch**. Soon in the distance will be seen the slender spire of the church. Keep straight on to pass Fairfield High School on the right, then turn left at a T junction. At the next T-junction turn left on the B4348 to shortly arrive in Peterchurch. Turn left beside the *Boughton Arms* if you wish to visit the church. There is a car park on the right.

*The noble spire of the fine Norman Church rises grandly in the midst of the valley, the white houses of the village are gathered round it and hard by are one or two poplars rising with golden green spires against the blue sides of the distant hills. The Church is approached over a broad rude stone pitched causeway, quaint and ancient, which borders and then bridges the broad fair stream of the Dore which flows close beneath the churchyard and the green steeple of St Peter's Church. The Church is well restored but I was disappointed to find the old picture of the Peterchurch Fish gone from the interior wall. The picture of the Fish was on the wall furthest from the door as you go in. They do say the Fish was first seen at Dorstone and speared there, but he got away and they hunted him down to Peterchurch and killed him close by the Church. He was as big as a salmon and had a gold chain round his neck.*

Peterchurch in the Golden Valley has one of the tallest spires in England

Peterchurch can boast one of the tallest spires in England. Its impressive height of 186 feet is also unusual in the fact that the original stone spire, which became unsafe, was replaced in 1972 by a reinforced plastic one. A helicopter was used to lower it into position.

A Saxon timber church was founded on this site in 786 and replaced by a stone building by the Normans in about 1130. The only apparent remnant of the Saxon church is the ancient stone altar which is believed to be the oldest in England. It has been claimed that the stone was originally one of those at Arthur's Stone, a prehistoric burial chamber situated 1,000 feet above the valley. It is said to have been brought down from that site and consecrated as an altar top.

It is unusual that such a large church has no aisles, but it comprises a nave, two chancels and an apse which all date back to Norman times. Three Norman chancel arches lead eastward to the Norman window above the ancient altar stone. The first is a simple arch leading from the nave into the outer chancel. A second arch linking the outer, with the inner chapel, is ornate with bold chevron and zig zag decoration on its stones. The third arch leads from the inner chancel into the rounded apse.

Otherwise the interior of the church is plain and austere, but of special interest are its amazing accoustics. The faintest whisper of the priest standing by the centre of the altar can be heard clearly throughout the church. Everything that the priest says is echoed back to him a syllable late, but no-one else hears the echo at all.

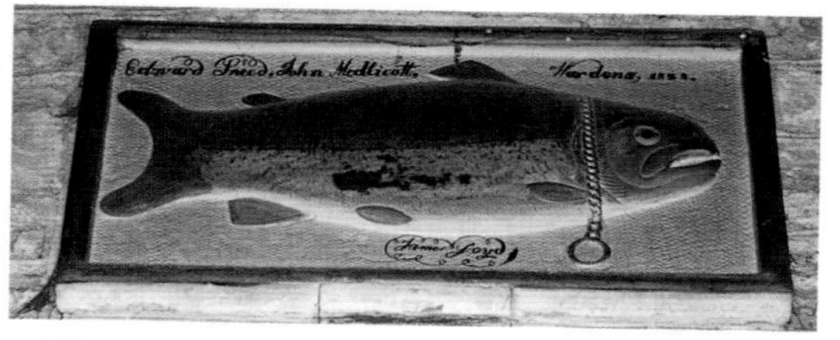


Plaster cast of the trout wearing a gold chain

High on the wall in the nave can be seen a plaster panel of a painted fish wearing a necklet. It is said to represent a trout which was caught in the River Dore by monks long ago. To their surprise they found that it was wearing a golden chain around its neck. Alternatively the trout, complete with gold chain, is said to have been found in St Peter's well, about half-a-mile from the church.

The churchyard is very spacious and one cannot help noticing the magnificent yew tree, some seven hundred years in age and 28 ft in circumference. It has seats curved around it, placed there so that people can sit in the shade.

One of the graves in the churchyard commemorates Robert Jones who won a VC in the Zulu War of 1879 and participated in the famous battle at Rorke's Drift, when a small detatchment of South Wales Borderers made a heroic stand against some 3,000 warriors.

The lofty 13th century tower has walls five feet thick at the top and was obviously designed to carry a substantial spire. The original one, 195 feet high was erected in about 1320. Five hundred and fifty years later it was restored at a cost of £700, but it then became unsafe and was taken down in 1945.

The fibre glass replacement (of 1972) can be seen the length and breadth of the valley, providing a fine landmark that pinpoints Peterchurch which is generally acknowledged as the 'capital' of the Golden Valley.

The grave of Robert Jones who won a VC during the Zulu War of 1879

After visiting the church return to the main road and turn left to follow the B4348 to **Dorstone**. When the road makes a sharp bend to the left turn right (signposted Bredwardine and Arthur's Stone). The road climbs steeply, flattens out and then descends towards Bredwardine. Shortly, turn left to follow a lane (signposted Arthur's Stone) which climbs back to the ridge and in due course Arthur's Stone, a prehistoric burial chamber will be seen on the left with a parking area provided.

Arthur's Stone is a Neolithic burial chamber (2000-3000BC), consisting of a large slab of sandstone supported by several vertical stones. In ancient times the whole structure would have been covered with a large mound of earth. The massive slab of sandstone is 18 ft long and originally rested on eleven upright stones, some of which have fallen. This is the only cromlech to be found in Herefordshire.

*Walked with E. Awdry to Arthur's Stone in the morning. On the way I visited Joseph Gwynne and Sarah Lewis. Joseph Gwynne told me that when he was a boy the great stone called Arthur's Stone was much longer than it is now. A hundred sheep could lie under the shadow of it. Also the stone stood much higher on its supporting pillars than it does at present, so high indeed that an ordinary-sized man could walk under it. Across the green lane and opposite the stone was a rock lying flat in the ground upon which were imprinted the marks of a man's knees and fingers. These marks were believed to have been made by King Arthur when he heaved this stone up on his back and set it upon the pillars.*

On leaving Arthur's Stone, keep straight on and then take the next turning on the left which descends into the valley to rejoin the B4348. Turn right and follow the road to Hardwicke, passing the church on the right.

**Holy Trinity, Hardwicke** is a Victorian Church in a parish which was created out of part of Clifford parish on the southern side of the Hay to Bredwardine road in 1853. The church was built in 1851 at a cost of £4,000. The founders were Mrs Penoyre, Rev. T. H. Penoyre and Mrs Napleton Penoyre. In Kilvert's time, Thomas William Webb was the Vicar of Hardwicke and in his spare time he took a keen interest in astronomy. He set up a simple observatory made of wood and canvas in the vicarage garden, from which he conducted an important series of experiments. These were published in 1859 under the title *Celestial Objects for Common Telescopes*. Kilvert paid a visit to Hardwicke and records having seen what he refers to as the *Great Meteor* from Webb's observatory.

Holy, Trinity, Hardwicke where the Vicar was a keen astronomer

On reaching a T junction turn left and return to Hay-on-Wye (2 ½ miles) on the B4348.

# CAR TOUR TO THE NORTH OF CLYRO

37½ miles (60 km)

*I felt I might wander about these hills all my life and never want for a kindly welcome, a meal, or a seat by the fireside.*

Rev Francis Kilvert

Above Clyro is a wild secretive area of hill country that remains relatively unchanged in charm and atmosphere since the days when Francis Kilvert tramped its narrow lanes, fragrant with roses and foxgloves. He caught its very special spirit and framed it in the pages of his *Diary*.

It is a fascinating area of wooded dingles threaded by a labyrinth of hedge lined lanes and punctuated with an assortment of hill farms and old cottages which bear such names as Gwernfythen, Llwyngwilliam, Wernypentre etc., so familiar to the rambling curate. He was made welcome everywhere and invited into oak-beamed and flagstone-floored kitchens for cups of tea and homemade delicacies.

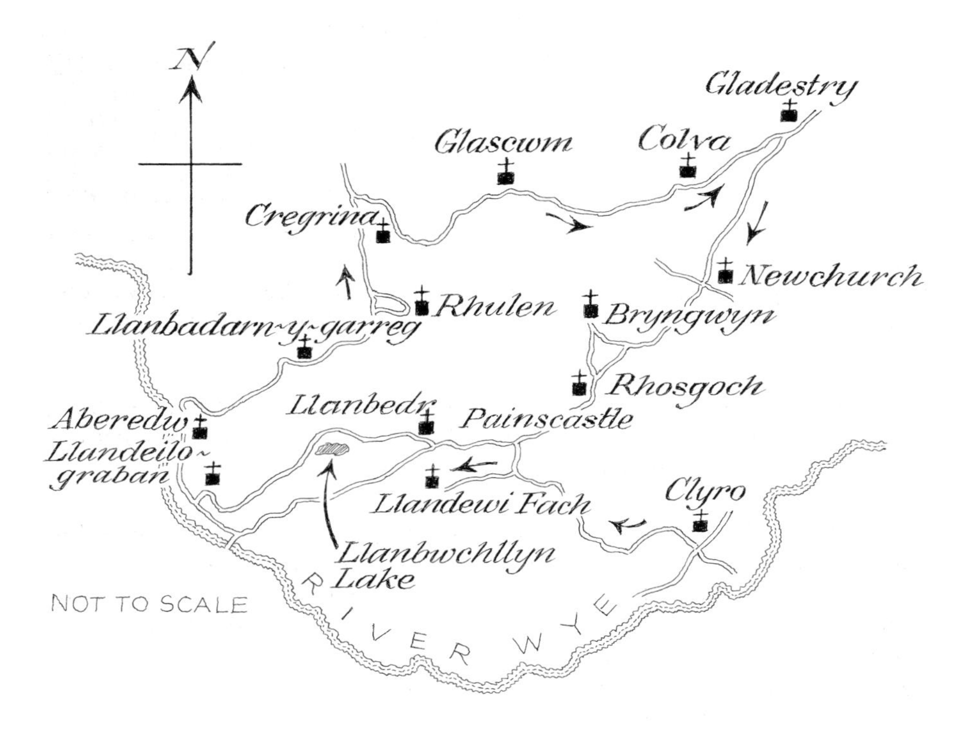

Follow the Painscastle road which starts on the west side of Clyro Church and ascend the hill, to soon leave the village behind. When the road levels out, turn left (signposted Painscastle 4 miles). Ignore the next turning on the left and the road continues to climb over a shoulder of the Begwyns. On crossing a cattle grid, the view ahead opens up dramatically. The Begwyns which rise to 1,361 feet and extend for about 2 miles from east to west, are often referred to by Kilvert as the 'Beacons'. This name stems from the time when Beacon fires were lit in high places as a means of raising alarm in times of war.

The Roundabout was named after a round plantation of trees which died after a severe winter in the late 1950s. From this fine vantage point is a 360 degree view of the Black Mountains, Brecon Beacons and the Radnor Hills. The drystone wall was restored in 1991 by Painscastle Community and the National Trust to celebrate the new millenium.

Continue down the hill towards Painscastle and the road now becomes narrower. If you wish to visit Llandewi Fach Church (GR146455), turn left at the bottom of the valley (signposted Llandewi Fach Church ¼ mile).

**Llandewi Fach** is a small church remotely situated in the hills to the south west of Painscastle and it may only be reached on foot from Cwm Farm. As the name implies, this church is dedicated to St David. Rebuilt in 1860 and re-roofed in 1963, it is a small building consisting of chancel, nave, south porch and a turret with two bells. The tiny nave contains two 17th century benches, while an unusual feature is the domestic style fireplace in the centre of the north wall.

Llandewi Fach is a remote little church that can only be reached on foot

Kilvert does not reveal if he visited this church, but he mentions the parish several times in his *Diary*. A small school was run in the church by the vicar, Mr Williams and Kilvert tells a story of Emma Williams, one of the pupils, who was attacked and nearly killed by a bull at Vron Ddu.

Return to the Painscastle Road and turn left. After crossing the Bachowey stream, the road climbs up to **Painscastle**. You may like to park on the left side of the road, opposite the bus shelter and take a stroll around the village.

In ancient times the old Welsh name for this remote settlement was Caer yn Elfael and it was probably a fort long before the medieval castle was built. A motte and bailey was established here in 1130 by Paganus de Cadurcis who accompanied the Conqueror into England and was given control of the Elfael which was a sub-province of the Welsh kingdom of Powys.

Paganus de Cadurcis was killed in a tournament in 1136 and his body taken to Gloucester to be interred in the Cathedral church by the side of his friend and ally Bernard de Neumarche who had led the conquest of Brycheiniog. A stone bears the inscription 'Hic jacet Pagunus de Cadurcis' - 'Here lieth Pain of Cahours'.

Part of the impressive earthworks of Painscastle

The original castle was completed by his son Thomas de Paganus who was also known as Fitz-Payn and it is from him that the place takes its name. His daughter and sole heir conveyed the castle to William de Braose, whose ancestor had married Bertha, grand-daughter of Bernard de Neumarche and daughter of Milo, Earl of Hereford. By virtue of that marriage William de Braose was created Lord of Brecknock and Buallt.

He rebuilt the castle and named it Castrum Matilus in honour of his wife, Maud de St Valerie. Towards the end of the 12th century a terrible battle took place here when Prince Gwenwynwyn besieged the castle in an act of revenge for the death of one of his relations at the hands of William de Braose. His cousin Trahaiarn on the orders of de Braose had been tied to the tail of a horse, dragged through the streets of Brecon and then beheaded. Gwenwynwyn, Prince of Powys was also a kinsman of Sytsyllt ap Dyfnwal who had been massacred with his retainers at a banquet held at Abergavenny Castle in December 1175. Following this foul deed William de Braose is remembered as the 'Ogre of Abergavenny'.

Gwenwynwyn, certainly had every reason to hate William de Braose and he swore an oath that he would sweep this Marcher Lord's dominions so bare with fire and sword that not a stick nor stone would be left standing within them. With a mighty army he marched on Painscastle to deal with William de Braose once and for all.

But the castle was well defended and the Norman baron had even persuaded one of the Welsh princes to raise the South against Gwenwynwyn and the men of Deheybarth and the Marcher Lords combined to destroy the army of this Prince of Powys. Gwenwynwyn was savagely defeated and three thousand of his men slain that terrible day.

In 1231 the castle was rebuilt by Henry III to be used as a base in the war against Llywelyn the Great. He built a round tower on the motte and a curtain wall with an east gatehouse and several other towers. For quite a few months he held court here, issuing a royal command to his subjects that they should destroy the wolves which were far more numerous and destructive in that area than in any other part of his realm.

Henry then left Painscastle under the command of Ralph de Tony, whose wife Petronella is remembered for beating off some Welsh invaders in 1250. History records that the last holders of the castle were the Earls of Warwick who garrisoned it against Owain Glyndwr in 1401.

But there is no remaining stonework of the once mighty castle to be seen now and its site is on private ground behind Castle Farm. It once covered about three acres but now there is nothing left but a huge mound, 27 ft high with a summit 66 ft long; a bailey 180 ft wide by 135 ft long and a deep surrounding ditch.

Sleepy Painscastle was once a thriving town with no less than six inns and when Kilvert came here in 1870 a mayor was still being elected annually. But Mr Price of Pendre Farm who held the office at that time sadly assured him that there were no longer any *emoluments, no dignity, and no powers.*

During the years of cattle droving Painscastle was an important stopping point on the route from Cardiganshire to England and more than 100,000 head of cattle a year passed through this little town. The six inns used to burst at the seams with thirsty cattle men and several forges did good business shoeing the cattle and the drovers' horses.

In order to walk the metalled roads cattle had to be shod with irons which in Wales were called *ciws* (cues in English). These were lighter than horseshoes and, of course adapted for cloven-hooves, so eight were required per beast. Each shoe was shaped like a crescent or a comma and every year thousands of these shoes were prepared by the blacksmiths in preparation for the droving season.

Kilvert was quite nostalgic for the *good old days of the drovers* and when he walked over Clyro Hill towards Crowther's Pool on May 3rd,1870, he *speculated upon the probable site of the Black Ox which was the house of call for the drovers of the great herds of black cattle from Shire Carmarthen and Cardigan on their way down into England.*

Painscastle village well, *the only one, which was formerly common and open to ducks and cattle had been neatly walled and railed round*

**Kilvert's first visit to Painscastle**

> *As we went up the steep hill to Painscastle the huge green Castle mound towered above us. A carpenter came down the hill from the village. I asked him where the grave of Tom Tobacco lay upon the moor, but he shook his head. He did not know.*
>
> *In the village, a Post Office had been established since I was last here and the village well, the only one, which was formerly common and open to ducks and cattle had been neatly walled and railed round. We went to Pendre, the house of the Mayor of Painscastle, but the Mayor was not at home.*

*At last Mr Price the Mayor was discovered in the centre of a group of village politicians before the alehouse door where:*

*While village statesmen talked with looks profound*
*The weekly paper with their ale went round.*

*Tom Williams talked to the Mayor about quarrying stone for the Painscastle school while the blacksmith leaned over the wall taking part in the conversation and the rest of the village statesmen lounged in the inn porch. The Mayor came up with us on to Llanbedr Hill to show us the best quarry.*

*He said Painscastle was an old broken borough, one of the Radnorshire boroughs, and they still went through the form of electing one of the chief men of the village as Mayor. Sometimes the office ran in one family for some time. Williams asked the Mayor if he had any power. 'No', answered that dignity, 'I dinna think I have much power.' We stopped to look at the stone of the ruined village pound. With a touch of dry humour the Mayor told us that at the last Court Leet the village authorities and tenants of the Manor had made a present to the Lord of the Manor (Mr de Winton) of the pound, the stop gate and the village well, that he might keep them in repair. Pointing to one of his fields, whose boundary had lately been moved and enlarged, he said with a merry twinkle in his eye, 'Because the Lord had not land enough before I have taken in a bit more for him off the waste.' The Mayor said there was a small school kept near Llanbedr Church by an old man, who taught the children well. 'But I do consait he do let them out too soon in the evening he do', said the Mayor disapprovingly.*

*The Mayor took us to the quarry and discoursed without enthusiasm and even with despondency on the badness of the roads, the difficulty of hauling the stone and the labour of 'ridding' the ground before the stone could be raised. After some talk at the quarry about ways and means, we parted, the Mayor returning to his mayoralty which had no emolument, no dignity, and no powers, he 'didna think,' and we going on over the hill towards the abode of the hermit.*

Let us now continue with our car journey. Keep straight on along the B4594 and in due course Llanbedr Church will be seen directly ahead, below a tree crowned hill. Take a turning on the right (signposted Llanbedr Church ¼ mile). Park near the top gate to the churchyard, opposite Hall Farm.

**Llanbedr Painscastle Church** (GR 141464) is situated about 2 miles west of Painscastle in the valley of Bach Howey. It is a 13th century church, with a 15th century chancel, nave, porch and a low tower containing three bells. In Kilvert's time this church was virtually a ruin and restoration did not take place untill 885. The large churchyard of 2 acres is circular, and just like many others in Radnorshire there are no graves on the north side, for that was the domain of the Devil! The circular base of the old churchyard cross can be seen and in the porch is a 13th century water stoup.

Llanbedr-Painscastle stands in a circular churchyard and the vicar here in Kilvert's time was the Rev John Price

There is an excellent local history display inside the church relating to the history of the building, its locality and its one-time eccentric vicar, the Rev John Price. This classical scholar of Queen's College, Cambridge was vicar of Llanbedr from 1859 to 1895. He was about sixty when Kilvert met him in 1872 and had luxuriant chestnut hair and moustache and a white beard. He wore a greasy black dress coat, broken shoes, a large cravat and a tall hat.

When he became vicar of this parish in 1859, there was no vicarage provided, and his stipend was so meagre that he had to make do with the most basic of accommodation. He first resided in a small croft (Pencwm) until forced to move and then set up home in three old bathing machines which he had obtained from Aberystwyth and brought to this location. Known locally as 'The Huts' they served as his study, bed-room and kitchen.

One day a tramp got into the huts and searched for money but found none and carried away a parcel instead. To his disappointment he found that it only contained letters which had been written to Price by a young lady many years previously. In anger he tore them up and scattered the pieces around the common. John Price was seen during the following fortnight out in the rain and wind, wandering around the common seeking the remains of his letters, which were obviously of sentimental value to him.

It was shortly after this incident that the huts and all his possessions were destroyed by fire and he was reduced to living in the whitewashed henhouse where Kilvert found him on 3rd July, 1872.

The grave of the Rev John Price can be seen just beyond the porch

The Rev John Price was certainly an unusual clergyman. He was a farmer's son and had been born near Llandeilo in Carmarthenshire. After graduating in Classics at Queen's College, Cambridge, he then held curacies in various parts of England before coming down from Gorton, Lancashire, in 1859 to take the living of Llanbedr-Painscastle which had been vacant for seven years.

Most of his parishioners were dissenters and did not attend church. So he made an offer of sixpence per head per service (later when he lost his private income, this had to be reduced to twopence). In this way he began to fill his pews with unwashed tramps and further enticement in winter involved the provision of oil stoves. Cooking was even allowed during the sermon.

Price also offered five shillings to each pair of vagrants 'living in sin' who would consent to let him join them in Holy Wedlock. As his sight was poor, several sly couples let him marry them half a dozen times.

John Price certainly did not look after himself at all well and near the end of his life, his health was made even worse by an accident which befell him. This incident was described to Kilvert by Mrs Price (of Monnington Mill), who used to live near Coed y Garth above Llanbedr Church.

*He was sitting by the fire in his little lone hut at Cwm Cello that lies in the bosom of Llanbedr Hill when he either dropped heavily asleep or had a fit and fell full upon the fire. Before he could recover himself his stomach, bowels and thighs were dreadfully burnt, and he has had to stay away from Church for three Sundays. Yet he will let neither doctor nor nurse come near him. The poor solitary. He used to visit Sarah Bryan kindly and assiduously when she lay a-dying and was a great and lasting comfort to her. She died happy.*

Eventually Price sank into an appalling state of neglect and was taken by friends to Talgarth Hospital, where it was found necessary to cut his clothes away from his skin. The bath that followed, must have been too much for him and he died in his sleep that night, aged eighty-six. Three days later, on 23rd March, 1895, he was buried in Llanbedr-Painscastle churchyard. His grave near the south door of the church is marked by a white cross bearing the words 'For me to live is Christ and to die is gain.'

## WALK 7

### *To the site of the Solitary's Hut in Penycwm*

4 miles (6.4km)

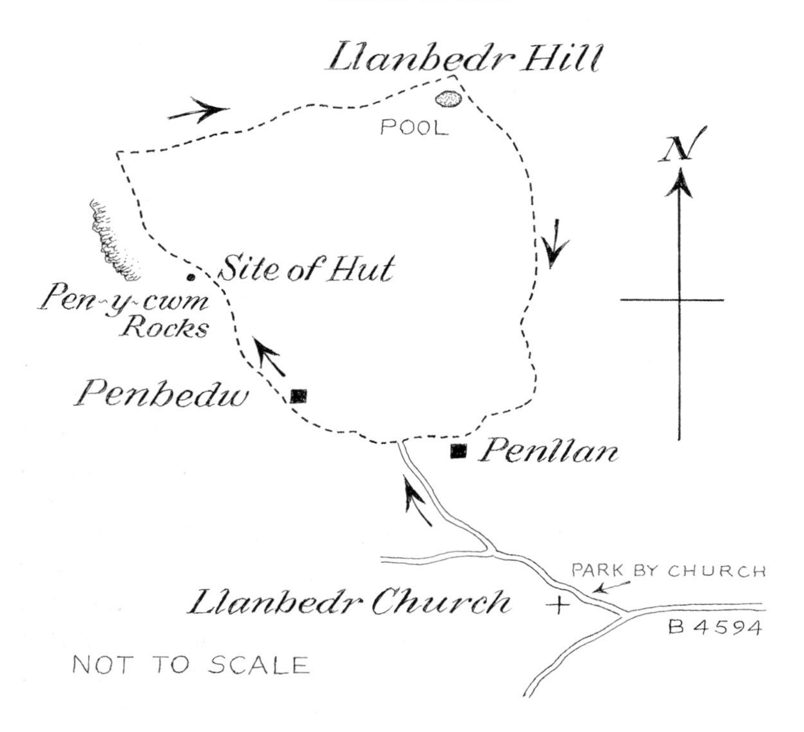


From Llanbedr Church walk up the road for about ¼ mile and take the first turning on the right. A steady ascent brings you to a gate across the road. Pause for a moment to look back at the view towards the Black Mountains and then continue with the Pen-y-cwm rocks now seen directly ahead just below the skyline. The cluster of buildings across to the right is Penllan Farm.

On reaching a T-junction turn left and follow the hedge lined road to Penbedw Farm. Here the tarmac ends but a stony track continues through the farmyard gates. The valley ahead seems wild and remote - just the place for a man of a solitary disposition to reside.

It was on 3rd July, 1872 that Kilvert tramped over the hills from Clyro with his friend Tom Williams, Vicar of Llowes, to call on the Rev John Price. This eccentric vicar of Llanbedr-Painscastle was living like a hermit in a hut of drystone walling and leaking thatch, situated in a secluded cwm below Llanbedr hill.

*At length we came in sight of a little hollow, a recess in the hills at the foot of Llanbedr Hill, a little cwm running back into the mountain closed at the end and on both sides by the steep hill sides but open to the South, and the sun and the great valley of the Wye and the distant blue mountains. A sunny green little cwm it was secluded deep among the steep green hills, and until you came close to it you would not be suspecting the existence of the place. A well watered little cwm with sweet waters from the upper and lower springs which welled up through the turf and peat and fern and heathers, and joining their rills trickled away in a tiny stream down the cwm to form a brook.*

*In this green cwm stood a little grey hut. It was built of rough dry stone without mortar and the thatch was thin and broken. At one end of the cabin a little garden had been enclosed and fenced in from the waste. There was one other house in sight where the cwm lay open to the west, Pencommon which used to belong to Price, the old keeper, who died lately in Clyro Village. Not a soul was stirring or in sight on the hill or in the valley, and the green cwm was perfectly silent and apparently deserted. As we turned the corner of the little grey hut and came in sight of the closed door we gave up all hope of seeing the Solitary and believed that our pilgrimage had been in vain. Then what was my relief when I knocked upon the door to hear a strange deep voice from within saying, 'Ho! Ho!' There was a slight stir within and then the cabin door opened and a strange figure came out. The figure of a man rather below the middle height, about 60 years of age, his head covered with a luxuriant growth of light brown or chestnut hair and his face made remarkable by mild thoughtful melancholy blue eyes and red moustache and white beard. The hermit was dressed in a seedy faded greasy suit of black, a dress coat and a large untidy white cravat, or a cravat that had once been white, lashed round his neck with a loose knot and flying ends. Upon his feet he wore broken low shoes and in his hand he carried a tall hat. There was something in the whole appearance of the Solitary singularly dilapidated and forlorn and he had a distant absent look and a preoccupied air as if the soul were entirely unconscious of the rags in which the body was clothed.*

Kilvert was considerably shocked by the conditions in which this well educated man was living and he described Price's squalid residence as follows:-

*The house was a sight when once seen never to be forgotten... Inside the hut there was a wild confusion of litter and rubbish almost choking and filling up all available space. The floor had once been of stone but was covered thick and deep with an accumulation of the dirt and peat dust of years. The furniture consisted of two wooden saddle-seated chairs polished smooth by the friction of continual sessions, and one of them without a back. A four-legged dressing table littered with broken bread and meat, crumbs, dirty knives and forks, glasses, plates, cups and saucers in squalid hugger-mugger confusion. No table cloth. No grate. The hearth foul with cold peat ashes, broken bricks and dust, under the great wide open chimney through which stole down a faint ghastly sickle light. In heaps and piles upon the floor were old books, large Bibles, commentaries, old fashioned religious disputations, C.M.S. Reports and odd books of all sorts, Luther on the Galatians, etc.*

The little stone hut in a secluded cwm below Llanbedr Hill, where the Rev John Price lived like a hermit

*The floor was further encumbered with beams and logs of wood, flour pans covered over, and old chests. All the other articles of food were hung up on pot hooks from the ceiling, some in the chimney out of the way of the rats. The squalor, the dirt, the dust, the foulness and wretchedness of the place was indescribable, almost inconceivable. In this cabin thus lives the Solitary of Llanbedr, the Revd John Price, Master of Arts of Cambridge University and Vicar of Llanbedr Painscastle.*

The track continues through a couple of gates and then bends to the right around the edge of a field. Just beyond the next gate and near the base of a small quarry will be found the site of the 'Solitary's hut'. But all that can be seen now is just a few stones at the right hand end of the quarry.

Either retrace your steps or continue to complete a circular walk by following the old quarry track to the head of the valley. When reaching the ridge turn right along a broad track leading along Llanbedr Hill. The views are extensive on a clear day.

After about 1 mile turn right down a track leading past a small round pool (sometimes dry). Soon you will pass a disused quarry on the left and in due course the track goes through a gap between two fences, through a gate and then more steeply down into the valley.

The track develops into a stony cart road accompanied by a stream on the left. A gate is reached and then after crossing a stream go right to pass above Penllan Farm where you join a road leading to a junction and your outward route. Turn left and follow the road back to Llanbedr Church.

Pen-y-cwm Rocks is the place *where the fairies were last seen*

## Continuation of Car Tour

From Llanbedr Church continue along the narrow lane which ascends gently to reach a point where the view opens out to the right towards Penycwm (site of the 'Solitary's Hut'). As the road descends, Llan Bwch-llyn, the largest pool in Radnorshire will come into view for a brief moment before being obscured by trees.

> *Then there was a gleam of silver over the dark heather stems and Llanbychllyn Pool lay in its hollow like a silver shield. The view was beautiful and we all lay down upon the dry heather just budding into pink blossom to enjoy the fair and 'delicate prospect' in full view of the grey rocks and silver lake. And the curlews called and the plovers whistled with their strange wild whistle about the sunny hill.*

Llanbwchllyn (Buckgrove Lake) the largest pool in Radnorshire, is situated 962 feet above sea level and about 10 acres in area. It is the centre of many superstitions and stories and was even mentioned by Giraldus Cambrensis in his *Itinerary* when he claimed that this mysterious pool had shifted its position two miles in a single night. There is also a legend that a maiden bathing in the lake was seized and carried off to Painscastle. She escaped disguised as a soldier but was shot by her lover, who failed to recognise her.

## WALK 8

### *To Llanbwychllyn Lake*

¼ mile (0.4 km)

Just before Llanbwchllyn Farm, a small gate on the left gives access to the lake and a bird watchers' hide. This Site of Special Scientific Interest is managed by the Radnorshire Wildlife Trust. Parking by the gate is rather limited with space only for about two cars or one minibus.

A level path leads down through the trees to the lakeside hide and access beyond that point is restricted to fishermen with permits. Birds recorded here include: Great Crested Grebe, Mallard, Teal, Pochard, Coot, Moor Hen, Heron, Curlew, Dunlin and Sandpiper. Mute Swans also breed on the lake.

>>>>>>>>>>>>>>>><<<<<<<<<<<<<<<<

### Continuation of the Car Tour

Drive on, ignoring the next turning on the left. Keep straight on (following road signposted Llandeilo 1 ½ miles). As the road climbs, the views open up towards the Black Mountains and from the brow of a hill, the view extends to the other side of the Wye Valley.

Turn left just before a red telephone box and stop shortly by some buildings on the left to visit **Llandeilo Graban Church** (GR 094446). Founded by St Teilo in the sixth century, this church is situated within a circular graveyard, from which there are magnificent views. The present building is largely 14th century and consists of chancel, nave and south porch. The registers date from 1696.

There is a local tradition that the last dragon of Radnorshire met its dramatic end at this location. This creature terrorised the district during the day time and adopted the habit of sleeping the night away on top of the church tower. Local folklore relates that it was a ploughboy who managed to rid the county of this frightening beast.

He made a dummy man out of a large log, and, aided by the local blacksmith, armed it with numerous iron hooks, powerful, keen and barbed. Then he dressed the dummy in red and fixed it firmly on top of the tower. At dawn the following day the dragon first saw his daring bedfellow, and dealt him a violent blow with his tail, which was badly torn by the hooks. Infuriated by the pain, he attacked the dummy with tooth, claw, wing and tail, then finally wound himself round his wooden foe, and bled to death.

Llandeilo Graban was founded by St Teilo in the sixth century

Continue along the road to join the B4594. Turn right (signposted Erwood 1 ¾ miles). The road snakes around a series of hair-pin bends to reach the bottom of the valley. Turn right to follow the B4567 (signposted Aberedw 3 ½ miles).

Shortly on the left is Erwood Station Craft Centre. This old railway station is a good place to stop for a refreshment break, visit the toilets or perhaps view an exhibition of paintings.

From here the road runs parallel with the old Mid Wales Railway which was frequently used by Kilvert when travelling to visit the Venables family at Llysdinam, near Newbridge-on-Wye.

Follow the road to reach a turning on the right (signposted Aberedw) and on reaching the village park near the *Seven Stars Inn*.

**Aberedw** is a delightful hamlet situated near the mouth of the Edw which rises in the moors of Llandegley and flows down a narrow and beautiful valley to join the Wye.

Founded by St Cewydd, Aberedw Church (GR 080473) stands on an ancient site but is mainly 14th century and was much restored in 1868. An interesting feature is the spacious timber porch constructed of substantial oak beams and with seats along its sides, where musicians used to sit and play while village folk danced in the churchyard. Such merriment especially took place on the day of the village feast held on 7th July which is the anniversary of the Translations of St Thomas of Canterbury.

Aberedw Church  was founded by St Cewydd in the 6th century

Aberedw Castle was built in a commanding position above the River Edw

Aberedw is famous for its associations with Prince Llywelyn ap Gruffydd (the last native Prince of Wales) who is said to have spent his last night alive sleeping in a cave (GR 084467) among the rocks above the village. This simple rock shelter is known as Llywelyn's Cave, although there is a tradition that it was first used by St Cewydd who founded Aberedw Church. For centuries the field adjoining the cave has been known as Cae Cewydd.

A story is often told of how Prince Llywelyn, knowing that his English pursuers were not far away, had the village blacksmith reverse the shoes on his horse's hooves to lay a false trail in the snow. Unfortunately the blacksmith turned traitor and told Edward Mortimer (who was commanding the English force) of the deception. In due course Llywelyn heading back towards Aberedew rode into a band of English soldiers at Cilmeri, just outside Builth and was killed by one named Adam Frankton.

Llywelyn ap Gruffydd had a small castle at Aberedew which he used as a hunting lodge. The remnants of this stronghold with its four round towers was finally destroyed when the Cambrian Railway (long closed) was constructed through the site and stones from the building broken up to ballast the track between Aberedw and Llanelwedd.

Another castle site in the form of a motte and bailey can also be seen on high ground in a strong defensive position with a sheer drop of 150 feet to the river Edw on its south western side. This is said to have been built by Sir Radulphus de Baskerville, Lord of Yerdisley (Eardisley) whose family invaded England with William the Conqueror.

During the reign of Henry II, Sir Radulphus Baskerville of Aberedew married Drago a daughter of Lord Clifford of Clifford Castle. Soon afterwards a dispute over some land ownership resulted in these two men settling the matter by fighting a duel. Lord Clifford was killed and Sir Radulphus in an act of conscience later bought a pardon from the Pope. This was given, not as one might expect, for killing his father-in-law, but for performing the savage deed in a churchyard!

Kilvert was entranced with Aberedw and particularly impressed by the bold outcrops of rock which rise terrace upon terrace, for 700 feet above the river, with their summits crowned with bush, scrub and trees. On these walls and pinnacles of Silurian limestone can be seen the marks of Britain's big freeze-up in the Ice Age, when enormous glaciers came scraping and grinding down these valleys. This terraced formation which runs for about a mile above the Wye inspired Kilvert to write a rhapsody:

*Oh, Aberedew, Aberedew. Would God I might dwell and die by thee. Memory enters in and brings back the old time in a clear vision and waking dream, and again I descend from the high moor's half encircling sweep and listen to the distant murmur of the river as it foams down the ravine from its home in the Green Cwm and its cradle in the hills. Once more I stand by the river side and look up at the cliff castle towers and mark the wild roses swinging from the crag and watch the green woods waving and shimmering with a twinkling dazzle as they rustle in the breeze and shining of the summer afternoon, while here and there a grey crag peeps from among the tufted trees. And once again I hear the merry voices and laughter of the children as they clamber down the cliff path among the bushes or along the rock ledges of the riverside or climb the Castle Mount, or saunter along the green meadow tree-fringed and rock-bordered and pass in and out of Llewellyn's cave, or gather wood and light the fire among the rocks upon the moor, or loiter down the valley to Cavan Twm Bach and cross the shining ferry at sunset, when the evening shadows lie long and still across the broad reaches of the river. Oh, Aberedew, Aberedew.*

The River Wye from Aberedw Rocks, engraved by S. Lacey, after H. Gastineau, 1830

## WALK 9

### *To Prince Llywelyn's Cave*

1 ¼ miles (2 km)

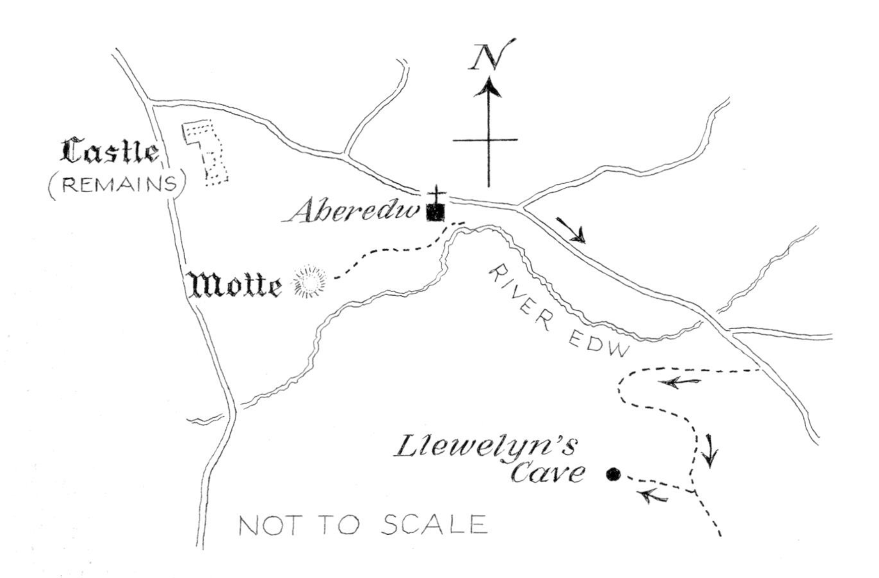


From Aberedw church follow the road down to a junction. Keep right of the telephone box and shortly cross the River Edw on a stone bridge. Turn right up a lane and after about 100 yards (90 metres) turn right again, to follow a rough track through a gate. It rises up through the trees and then bends sharply to the left.

Shortly after passing through a gate, go right through a gap on the right. Walk around the edge of a field for about 100 yards and then turn left past the remains (at time of writing) of a small wooden gate. A path leads a short distance to Prince Llywelyn's Cave, which is is well concealed in the trees.

> *About a hundred yards from the road amongst the rocks and bushes was Llewellyn's Cave with a door. We went in. There was a step down into it and the Cave was a square dark small chamber just high enough to stand upright in, and at the further dark end a hole or shaft probably a chink in the rocks up which we could thrust our arms and sticks without feeling the end. Naves were carved on the walls.*

Prince Llywelyn ap Gruffyd is said to have spent his last night alive in this very small rock shelter in December 1282 when pursued by English soldiers. Inside, the walls are scratched with the names and dates of some of the many visitors who have been here over the years.

There is a legend that a local blacksmith reversed the shoes on the hooves of Llywelyn's horse so that the tracks in the snow would mislead his enemies. However, the blacksmith then sold this information to the English troops. Prince Llywelyn was caught and beheaded at Cilmeri, near Builth Wells.

Retrace your steps back to Aberedw.

Llywelyn's Cave is quite small, about 6 feet square with a very small entrance. There is a small peep-hole 2 feet by 6 inches in the right-hand corner. It is possible that this cave which was used for peaceful prayer and meditation in the 6th century by Cewydd, gave Prince Llywelyn a few hours shelter on that snowy night in December, 1282, the night before he fell, and with him went the independency of Wales. The field adjoining the cave has been known for centuries as Cae Cewydd (Cewydd's Field).

Drive on from Aberedw to follow the road through the narrow and beautiful Edw valley, leading back into the hills. Stop just before a stone bridge and go through a kissing gate to visit **Llanbadarn-y-garreg Church**. (GR 112487), a small whitewashed building situated in a green meadow beside the rushing Edw. This simple church was built in the 13th or 14th centuries. It has an old font, a rood beam and a 15th century screen with a faded painting.

Llanbadarn-y-garreg stands in a peaceful spot beside the River Edw

The road now ascends for a while above the river and then drops down to pass Hergest Bridge. Carry on to reach a T junction. Turn right here (signposted Rhulen ½ mile). Shortly, turn left along a narrow lane to reach **St David's Church at Rhulen** (GR 137498).

Guarded by several ancient yews, the churchyard is circular and may well have once been a pre-Christian burial ground. This little white-washed church dates from the 12th century and consists of a nave and wooden belfry. It has seating accommodation for about forty people. The registers date from 1763 and the living is annexed with Colva to that of Glascwm.

Some enlargement took place during the 14th century and the church was re-roofed in 1961-2, using stone tiles as in the original Norman construction. The west wall was taken down in 1987, having developed an unhealthy lean and it was rebuilt using the same stones. No screen was ever installed in this church, but the heavy beams over the altar originally supported the rood. The font bowl is 14th century and stands on an older base.

St David's Church, Rhulen (137498) is situated on a hillside two miles south of Cregrina. The name in old Welsh is Rhiwlyn and it is derived from a brook which flows through the valley of Rhulen and once provided the power for a nearby corn mill.

The porch seems large for the size of the church and in earlier times it would have been used for parish meetings and sometimes for the first part of the marriage service. Of particular interest is the sanctuary ring to the left of the handle of the church door. It recalls the time long ago when people wanted for various crimes could claim sanctuary in a church for up to forty days. Giraldus Cambrensis mentions that sanctuary applied 'not only in churchyards but outside, too, within the fences and ditches marked out and set by the bishops to fix ... the limits'. The right of sanctuary was abolished in the seventeenth century.

Leaving Rhulen with regret for it is a delightful place, now descend into the valley and drive up the other side. Ignore a turning to the right and follow the hedge-lined lane which takes you ever deeper into the heart of *Kilvert Country*. On reaching a T junction, turn right along a wider road, passing above a wooded valley in which during the reign of Elizabeth I , the last wolf in Radnorshire was shot. The paws of this unfortunate animal were nailed to the door of nearby Cregrina Church.

The road drops down, ignore the turning to the right and continue to reach the hamlet of Cregrina. Park by a red telephone box on the left. Situated beside a musical stretch of the river Edw, the hamlet of **Cregrina** has been a quiet sleepy place since the cattle drovers ceased to pass this way. It is believed that the name of this settlement is of Goidelic origin and connected with a St Runa (Ceryg Runa).

St Davids Church in the hamlet of Cregrina

Walk a few yards up the road on the left of the telephone box and follow a grass path leading up to **St David's Church** (GR 123521), which is perched on a level area of ground overlooking the Edw.

Consisting of porch, nave, chancel and a low tower, this church is largely 13th century. The screen has survived but the rood above it depicting Christ on the Cross, with St Mary and St John standing on either side has long been removed.

Both Cregrina and Rhulen are daughter churches to Glascwm which was once important in medieval church affairs. Cregrina Church was restored in 1958 with the help of a grant from the Pilgrim Trust.

Now drive on through the village, passing the 'Cregrina Free Mission' on the right with the 'Old Vicarage' next door. The lane climbs out of the village and then descends with views into distant Radnorshire.

*The beautiful Glasnant came leaping and rushing down its lovely dingle, a flood of molten silver and crystal fringed by groups of silver birches and alders...*

On reaching a T junction, turn right for Glascwm (3 miles). Cross a stone hump-backed bridge and follow the road twisting and turning, alternately climbing and descending, to reach **Glascwm**.

Park in the village by the red telephone box opposite the old school. This peaceful village, where time seems to have called a halt, is situated in the valley of the Clas (as the name implies) and it was once an important stopping place for drovers on their way from Cardiganshire into England. As a result there were once several inns in the village, including the *Drovers Arms*, the *Radnorshire Arms*, the *Carpenters Arms*, the *Masons Arms* and the *Beavan Arms*. Now there is not a single hostelry and in recent years even the once popular Youth Hostel (the old school) has closed.

Walk back up the road a short way and follow a gravel path on the right to reach the church which is dedicated to St David (GR 156532) and stands in a banked curving churchyard. The building has a large timber bell-cote and according to Giraldus Cambrensis this church used to possess a handbell which had the most miraculous powers. It was supposed to have belonged to St David. Giraldus came here in 1188, when he was accompanying Archbishop Baldwin on their famous journey around Wales, seeking Welsh support for the Third Crusade. Thoroughly restored in 1891 the church now consists of chancel, nave, a south porch and a turret with one bell. The registers go back to 1679.

St David's, Glascwm, stands in a banked curving churchyard with sycamore lining the road above. It was thoroughly restored in 1891 and now consists of chancel, nave, south porch and a turret with one bell.

Kilvert describes his visit to this village in May 1871 when he called on Benjamin Marsden, who was vicar of Glascwm from 1851 to 1880:

> *First I went to the Vicarage. A pair of shears lay on the doorstep and a beautiful luxuriant briar climbed a trellis by the door and filled the whole porch with fragrance. I met the old Vicar magistrate in the hall with his stout frame, ruddy face, white hair, stern long sweeping eyebrows and a merry odd twinkle in his eye. One of the last old-fashioned parsons. He gave me some splendid Herefordshire cider and some bread and butter and there came in with him a very small black and tan terrier named Ti (for Tiger I suppose), a waddling gasping mass, a ball of fat.*
>
> *'I am bishop here,' said the Vicar. Then fetching the church key he added, 'Come and see the Cathedral'.*
>
> *The Cathedral lay a little distance down a pretty lane over arched and avenued with sycamores and limes. It was one of the very large Welsh Churchyards, 2 acres in extent and thinly peopled. The church long low and whitewashed, an unbroken line of roof without a tower or bell-turret of any kind. An immense chancel and an equally large belfry and a small nave. The belfry is the village school, fitted up with desks, forms and master's desk and a fireplace. The village clerk is village schoolmaster. In a huge deep Church chest were an old parish accounts book, an enormous flagon of pewter and pewter paten and a fragment of one of the Church bells. There used to be three good bells in Glascwm Church brought by the enchanted bisons from Llandewi Brefi. Just before the present Vicar came here there was a tremendous wedding of a farmer's daughter. There was great enthusiasm and excitement and the bells were required to ring very loud. One bell did not ring loud enough to satisfy the people so they took an axe up to the bell and beat the bell with the axe till they beat it to pieces.*

Benjamin Marsden was born in 1803 at Leek in Staffordshire, but was of Welsh background and could speak the language. When Kilvert met Marsden he had been a widower for some years, his wife Selina having died, aged 44, in 1853, just two years after their arrival in the parish. He was now living in the vicarage with an unmarried daughter and a servant.

In 1880 he resigned the living of Glascwm, having been in failing health for some time. His grave can be seen in the churchyard.

Continue along the road, climbing above Glascwm and where it levels out, the building on the left was once a pub called the *Three Wells*. On reaching a crossroads keep straight on (signposted Colva 1 mile). Then keep straight on again at the next minor crossroads to shortly pass a roadside sign informing you that you are entering **Colva**. But this hamlet is so small that if you blink you may miss it! The church will be seen shortly, just above the road on the left and there is just enough room to park a single vehicle by the entrance gate.

Situated at an altitude of 1,250 feet , **St David's** Church (GR 200531) is one of the most remote of all Radnorshire churches and one of the highest in Wales. The name is derived from Col, a sharp hillock or peak; and Fa, a place or Fach, little. The parish is situated near the source of the river Arrow, which runs through it, and borders it on the west for four miles.

Protected by four yew trees, the church is largely a 13th century construction with a deep 15th century south porch and a low doorway. On the partition wall separating the nave from the Belfry are the Royal Arms of King George III. They are inscribed *'1838 Thos. Davies Churchwarden. Cartwright de Aberedew, pinixit 1733'*.

The wooden belfry houses two bells, dated 1770 and 1740. Also of interest is the 13th century font which bears the hinge marks of its original cover.

St David's, Colva is one of the highest churches in Wales

Kilvert set out to walk to Colva on Saturday 26 February, 1870, in search of some folk songs that he had heard about and not having the use of a map he found it necessary to be guided there by a young boy whom he met at Green Lane Cottage:

> *A lovely warm morning so I set off to walk over the hills to Colva, taking my luncheon in my pocket, half a dozen biscuits, two apples and a small flask of wine. Took also a pocket book and opera glasses. Went on up Green Lane. Very hot walking. At the Green Lane Cottage found Mrs Jones and a daughter at home sewing. Price Price sitting half hidden in the chimney corner but alas there was no Abiasula as the last time I was there. Price Price something like his sister Abiasula. A sturdy boy, with a round good-humoured face and big black eyes, volunteered to guide me to Colva Church. So he came out of his chimney corner in the ingle nook and we started at once, accompanied by a grey and black sheepdog puppy. We were out on the open mountain at once. There was the brown withered heather, the elastic turf, the long green ride stretching over the hill like a green ribbon between the dark heather. There was the free fresh fragrant air of the hills, but, oh, for the gipsy lassie with her wild dark eyes under her black hood. As we went down the Fuallt a grouse cock uttered his squirling crow and flew over the crest of the hill. I never heard a grouse crow before. 'What's that bird crying?' I said to the boy. 'A grouse', he said, adding, 'There he goes over the bank. They be real thick hereabout.'*
>
> *Tried to get across the swift Arrow (swollen by the junction of the Glasnant just above) by climbing along a rail but we failed and had to go up a meadow till we got above the meeting of the waters, when we crossed the Glasnant on a hurdle laid flat over the stream and then we jumped the Arrow. Up the steep breast of the Reallt to Dol Realt and along the road to the Wern and Bryntwyn from whence a field path leads to Colva Church. Here Price Price left me after showing me across one field. I asked him to have some bread and cheese at the Sun Inn, Colva, but he would not and could scarcely be prevailed on to take sixpence. Tried the echo in the field against the belfry and west end of the poor humble dear little white-*

*washed church sequestered among its ancient yews. The echo was very clear, sharp and perfect. Richard Meredith told me of this echo.*

To test the echo go through the gate to the left of the churchyard gate. Walk up the field until you are level with the belfry, then turn left and walk for about 50 yards. Shout at the belfry and you will hear the echo, just like Kilvert - *very clear, sharp and perfect.*

Near the little church at Colva was the *Sun Inn* , used by drovers passing this way until the 1880s. Kilvert tells us how on the 26th February, 1870, he walked across the hills from Clyro and stopped at this inn to see Mr Phillips:-

*Mrs Phillips, the landlady of the Sun, was much frightened when I asked for her husband, uneasy and nervous lest I should have come to apprehend him for having been in a row or doing something wrong. But when I said I wanted the words of an old song, she was greatly relieved and said at once, 'Oh I know who you are. You are the gentleman from Clyro,' I laughed and she began to smile. Mrs Phillips took me into the parlour where I sat down, tore a leaf out of my pocket book and wrote with my address a request that Phillips would send me by post 1. the song about our Saviour, 2. the song about Lazurs, 3. the song about King James and the Tinker...*

A couple of miles south west of Colva, Kilvert paid a visit to Blaencerdi Farm where he was shown a jug from which King Charles I (Kilvert incorrectly says Charles II) had drunk milk during a hot journey in August 1645. The King was retreating with the remnants of his army after defeat at the Battle of Naseby and took this obscure route in order to avoid pursuit. The long train of horsemen riding two abreast, stretched over a mile along the narrow lanes and on that sweltering August day the King became tired and thirsty.

On reaching Blaencerdi Farmhouse, a mile beyond Newchurch he stopped to ask for a drink of milk. This was given to him by Mary Bayliss and he sat on a chair enjoying a brief rest. It was William Pritchard of Blaencerdi Farm, who showed Kilvert the jug from which the King had drank. With considerable pride, the family had preserved this piece of china through the centuries in memory of the King's visit.

From Colva, continue along this road to join the B4594 and descend into **Gladestry** which is situated in a beautiful fertile valley below Hergest ridge. This village is well known to walkers following the Offa's Dyke National Trail. The dyke (Clawdd Offa) was constructed by King Offa of Mercia in the 8th century to mark the boundary of his kingdom with Wales. You may like to obtain refrshments at the *Royal Oak Inn*.

**Gladestry Church** (GR 231552) is reputed to have been founded in 1060 by Harold who soon afterwards became King of England. But the authentic date is 1291, when the Rector was assessed at £5 6s 8d towards the costs of the Crusades against the Saracens. The stained glass windows are particularly fine. Built in local stone, the tower like those of many border churches was built as a place of refuge for the local inhabitants during times of trouble. It was altered in 1709 to make room for a peal of five bells and the rather quaint steeple was also added.

Gladestry Church was restored in 1910 and many of the old features preserved

Drive back up the hill and follow the B4594 towards Newchurch, which is about 3 miles away. As you get near this hamlet, you come over the brow of a hill and suddenly the Black Mountains and Brecon Beacons come into view. The road narrows as you drop steeply down into **Newchurch**, nestling in the bottom of this deep valley. Park near the entrance to the churchyard (GR 216508).

**St Mary's** was built in stone around the mid 1300s but there may have been a simple wooden church on the site before that time. The present structure was rebuilt in 1856.

Francis Kilvert often walked to Newchurch and he would have followed much of the route which is now designated as the Offa's Dyke National Trail.

*The day was lovely and I went over to Newchurch. A solitary fern cutter was at work on the Vicar's Hill mowing the fern with a sharp harsh ripping sound. From the Little Mountain the view was superb and the air exquisitiely clear. The Clee Hills seemed marvellously near. The land glittered, variegated with colours and gleams of wheat, stubble and blue hill. The yellow potentilla jewelled the turf with its tiny gems of gold and the frail harebell trembled blue among the fern tipped here and there with autumn yellow. The little lonely tree bowed on the mountain brow, and below lay the tiny village deep in the valley among the trees embosoming the little church with its blue spire and Emmeline's grave.*

Kilvert became a close friend of the Vaughan family who lived at Gilfach-yr-rheol. David Vaughan was the Vicar of Newchurch for 50 years but also found time to be a working farmer. Kilvert on one of his visits was perturbed to find two of the vicar's youngest daughters castrating lambs:-

*It was the first time I had seen a clergyman's daughters helping to castrate lambs or witnessing that operation and it rather gave me a turn of disgust at first. But I made allowance for them and considered how rough a way the poor children had been brought up, so that they thought no harm of it, and I forgave them.*

Emmeline Vaughan, one of the vicar's eldest daughters sadly died at the young age of 14 and on a later visit in March 1873, Kilvert mentions her grave in the churchyard:-

*As I stooped over the green grave by the churchyard gate, placing the primrose branches in a cross upon the turf, the large flakes of snow fell thickly upon us, but melted as they fell, and the great yew tree overhead bent weeping upon the grave.*

This magnificent yew tree was about 1,000 years old but it can no longer be seen for it was blown down during a hurricane in 1990.

St Mary's Newchurch where Kilvert's friend David Vaughan was vicar for 50 years

Grave of Emmeline Vaughan, who was just 14 when she died

Continue up the hill, following the Painscastle road (B4594) and take the second turning on the right (signposted Bryngwyn Church ¾ mile). The narrow lane leads up between high hedges to reach **St Michael's Church, Bryngwyn** (GR 186496). The church is dedicated to St Michael so the full Welsh name should be Llanfihangel y Bryn-gwyn.

St Michael's Church Bryngwyn

It was here that an old woman told Kilvert that on Easter morning she used to go to the Wild Duck Pool in the parish, *to see the sun dance and play in the water, and the angels who were at the Resurrection playing backwards and forwards below the sun.* She also told him that: *boys wore their caps back to front, so that they might not be enticed into fairy rings and made to dance.*

Turn left in front of the church to follow the lane down to rejoin the B4594 and turn right to shortly reach **Rhosgoch** (Red Marsh). Just before reaching this hamlet you will pass on the left an area of marsh or bog from which the place takes its name. It measures one mile and a quarter in length and half a mile in breadth. Excellent peat was extracted from it in days gone by and this fuel was said to be nearly equal in heat and durability to coal and even exceeded it in inflammability.

*Rhos Goch always seemed to me a place of magic and marvel. Strange birds haunted it, rare butterflies flitted above the heather, and the great osmunda ferns flowered there in myriads. There were different kinds of heath as well, and what the people called 'bog cotton' and 'burnt leaves', the latter an infallible cure for burns. Here, too were the lovely bog beans with their trefoil bean-like leaves, pink buds, and white blossoms fretted with exquisitively delicate filigree work, half like frosted silver and half like lace. Rhos Goch teemed with life. There were fish in the pools and on still warm summer afternoons you might hear the 'drumming' of the snipe as they circled in wild sweeps overhead. Wild duck bred among the pools; golden eye and curlew came there as well, and old people remembered when it had been a haunt of bittern. An old legend told of a dreadful battle which was fought at the western end of the Rhos, which caused the brook to run red with blood for three days, whence some people say the Common got its name of Rhos Goch (red bog).*

Rhos Goch - the 'Red Bog'

On the right will be seen the **Hermon Congregational Chapel**, which Kilvert viewed as a rival establishment. He described it as being *very ugly, high and boxy looking and of course whitewashed, the usual conventicle.*

Thomas Bayliss, the 65 year old village blacksmith, was in poor health when Kilvert visited him on 24th April 1872. He was born in Clifford and his wife Jane, who was of a similar age came from Winforton. Their son James, aged 25, was also a blacksmith. Thomas Bayliss is buried in the chapel graveyard but the inscription on his stone is now illegible. It used to read:

My sledge and hammer lie reclined
My bellows too has lost its wind
My fire's extinguished, my forge decayed
And in the dust my vice is laid
My coal is spent, my iron is gone
My nails are driven, my work is done.

Hermon Congregational Chapel at Rhosgoch

Further on , to the left of the road is the very overgrown **Rhosgoch Mill** which is situated on the Bachhowey Brook. Formerly, it was known as Hodenant Water Mill. The miller in Kilvert's day was William Powell who inherited the mill after his uncle died. This mill was run by the Powell family for over 400 years and William Powell earned himself the reputation of being a good grinder of wheat as well as cattle feed.

Rhosgoch Mill is described by Kilvert as picturesque with an overshot wheel and tall chimneys covered in ivy. It is still in the ownership of the Powell family, but one wonders - *are fairies still to be seen dancing of nights upon the mill floor ?*

*I decided to explore the lane running parallel with the brook towards Painscastle and discover old Rhos Goch Mill. There was a good deal of water and suddenly I came upon the mill pond and the picturesque old mill with an overshot wheel. I crossed one of the streams on a larch felled across the water for a bridge and came back round the front of the cosy old picturesque ivy-grown mill house with its tall chimney completely covered with ivy. A handsome young man with a fine open face, fresh complexion and dressed as a miller was having a romp with a little girl before the door. He said his name was Powell, his father was dead and he carried on the business and with the most perfect politeness and well bred courtesy asked me to come in and sit down. So this is the place that I have heard old Hannah Whitney talk of so often, the place where the old miller sleeping in the mill trough used to see the fairies dancing of nights on the mill floor.*

The road leads on back to Painscastle where you rejoin your outward route, thus completing this fascinating circuit in the hills above Clyro. As you follow the road back to your starting point in Clyro, ponder on the delightful scenery and places through which you have passed and marvel at the energy and enthusiasm of the Rev Francis Kilvert who spent so much time visiting the little churches and farms in this remote area. He thought nothing of walking twenty-five miles in a day and in the 1870s he would not have been following tarmac roads but just dusty cart tracks and muddy lanes full of pot holes.

# CAR TOUR OF THE UPPER WYE VALLEY

65 miles (104 km)

*I never had a lovelier journey up the lovely valley of the Wye. A tender beautiful haze veiled the distant hills and woods with a gauze of blue and silver and pearl. It was a dream of intoxicating beauty.*

Rev Francis Kilvert

Known by the Welsh as Afon Gwy and the Romans as Vaga (the wanderer - by reason of the frequent meanders of its course), the River Wye rises at a height of about 2,300 feet on the south-eastern side of Plynlimon in Montgomeryshire. For much of its course it has long served as a county boundary between Breconshire and Radnorshire. Towards the end of its journey, it divides Gloucestershire and Monmouthshire, while between these counties it flows through the middle of Herefordshire.

Kilvert often travelled by train up through the Wye Valley and this car tour explores the route that he would have known so well. He would have first walked a mile into Hay to catch a train to Three Cocks Junction. From there he took the Mid Wales Railway via Llechrhyd to Newbridge-on-Wye and sometimes as far as Rhyader.

The River Wye between Erwood and Builth Wells

Llowes Church was founded by St Meilig in the sixth century

From Clyro follow the A438 to **Llowes** (GR 194418), pronounced Hloughiss. The first church was founded by St Meilig who settled here in the sixth century. He was one of the many sons of Caw, who after serving as a soldier had turned to religion and studied under Cattwg at Llancarfan. One of his famous brothers was Gildas the monk historian and it is believed that St Meilig was buried within his simple building.

Today, this parish church which was rebuilt in 1853 by W. J. Worthington, consists of nave, chancel, south porch and an embattled western tower containing three bells. The font which probably dates back to about 1200 is encircled by iron bands because of a crack in the stone, and was probably installed in an earlier church on this site.

Also, of special interest in the church is the large stone cross-slab of St Meilig, which used to stand on the hillside above Llowes at a spot called Croesfeilig, where the parishes of Llowes, Clyro and Llanddewi Fach meet. In the twelfth century it was moved down to the churchyard where it stood for seven centuries. Then in 1956 the cross was taken inside the church in order to protect its carvings from further erosion by the elements. It is after all, the only carved cross in Radnorshire and the simple cross on one side has been ascribed to the 6th or 7th century, while the more elaborate Latin cross on the reverse side dates to the 11th century.

## Car Tour of the Upper Wye Valley

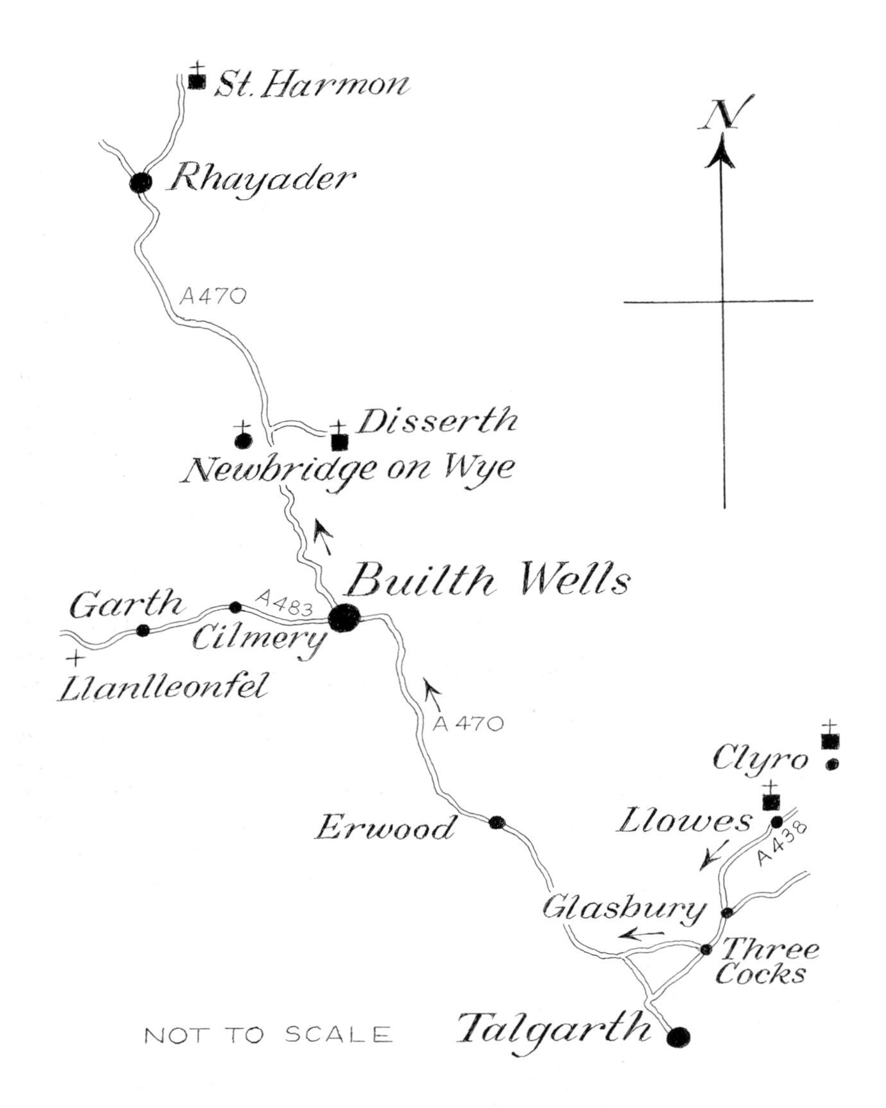

Local folklore refers to this cross-slab as Moll Walbee's Stone. This lady was Maud de Valeries, the stalwart spouse of William de Braose. It is said that she was carrying stones to rebuild Hay Castle (accomplished in a single night!) when one fell out of her apron and dropped into a her shoe. In anger she removed it and threw it across the Wye to land in Llowes churchyard.

The stone is also known as St Meulig's Cross and in the Dark Ages it stood on Bryn-yrhydd Common at a spot called Croesfeilig (St Meilg's Cross) to the north west of Llowes. In the 12th century it was removed from that location and installed in Llowes Churchyard, where it stood for about 800 years. In 1956 it was uprooted again and taken into the church to protect it from the elements. It is 7 feet high, 3 feet wide and 10 inches thick and weighs about 3 tons. It was probably originally a prehistoric standing stone that was converted into a Christian cross. The plain cross on its one face dates back to the 6th or 7th century while the more intricately decorated cross on the other face was carved in the 11th century.

In the churchyard by the path from the main gate is a sundial which was erected by the Kilvert Society in November 1954 to celebrate Francis Kilvert's close connection with this parish.

Vicarage House is an attractive two-storied stone building with a pillared porch. It was built by the Rev. Thomas Williams (Vicar 1859-1914) and Kilvert was often a visitor here. Thomas Williams MA was born at Llanvapley in Monmouthshire. He is buried by the gate at the east end of the churchyard. The 50th anniversary of his incumbancy was marked by the presentation to him of a Chalice and Pattern.

Kilvert makes several mentions of the Rev Tom Williams in the *Diary*. For example we hear of Tom Williams at a Llanthomas garden party in September 1871 and a few days later he is playing croquet with Kilvert and his sisters at Cae Mawr. Of particular interest is Kilvert's account of how he and Tom Williams paid a visit to 'the Solitary' at Llanbedr, Painscastle:

> *Tom Williams and I had long been talking of going up to Llanbedr Hill to pay a visit to the eccentric solitary, the Vicar, and we arranged to go this morning. The day promised to be fine and after school at 10.30 I walked over to Llowes. When the postman, who followed me closely, had arrived we started up a steep stony narrow lane so overgrown and over arched with wild roses that it was difficult for a horseman to pass, but a lane most beautiful and picturesque with its wild luxuriant growth of fern and wild roses and foxgloves. The foxgloves were wonderful, they grew on both sides of the lane, multitudes in long and deep array.*

*Tom Williams was on horseback, I on foot. As we mounted the hill, beautiful views of mountains and valley opened gleaming behind us, and Tom Williams pointed out to me some of the Llowes farmhouses scattered over the hills...All the folk were busy in their hay fields. Here and there my fellow pilgrim spoke to a labourer or small farmer over the hedge.*

Leaving Llowes continue along the A438 and you may find it of interest to make a brief detour to visit **Maesyronen**, one of the earliest Nonconformist chapels in Wales (GR 177411). Take the next turning on the right (signposted Maesyronen).

Maesyronen Chapel (GR 177411) stands on a steep hill above the Wye and is built on land bequeathed by Lewis Lloyd in 1686. It is one of the earliest Nonconformist chapels in Wales. The low single-storey building has a tiny cottage at one end and is still fitted with its seventeenth-century furniture, of the Commonwealth period.

Return to the A438 and turn right. After about a mile you will reach **Glasbury** (pronounced Glazebury), known in Welsh as Y Clas-ar-Wy, meaning the grange (or glebe) on the Wye. Situated close to the river, this village was once known as Gwladys Burh, being named after a daughter of Brychan Brycheiniog, who ruled these parts in the fifth century.

Glasbury Bridge marks the boundary between Breconshire and Radnorshire

It was here in 1055 that Gruffydd of Gwynedd, who burned Hereford, inflicted a crushing defeat on the Earl of Hereford (Ralph), the nephew of Edward the Confessor.

It is a large scattered village occupying both sides of the Wye which means it stands in both the old counties of Breconshire and Radnorshire and the parish once extended from The Gospel pass between Hay Bluff and Lord Hereford's Knob to the Begwns near Painscastle. The site of its first church is marked by a few mounds called the 'Stances', just visible on your right as you cross Glasbury bridge. It was abandoned in 1600 after the Wye changed its course following a great flood and the stones were used in the construction of a new church on higher ground on the Breconshire side of the river. Subsequently, complete rebuilding of this church took place in 1662-5 This remained the parish church for the whole of Glasbury on both sides of the Wye until 1882, when a new parish was created for the Radnorshire side of the river and the present ugly Gothic **St Peter's Church** (GR 177386) was constructed by Lewis Vulliamy at a cost of £3,000.

Kilvert tells us that an infant girl born in Glasbury was baptised Mahalah. The mother declared this to be the name of one of Cain's wives. An older daughter was Thirza, named after Cain's other wife.

It would appear that Kilvert once had hopes of becoming vicar of St Peter's, Glasbury, for an entry in his *Diary* on 22 September, 1871 reveals that: *Rev Welby asked why I had not got the living of Glasbury. He had hoped to hear of my being there.* The living instead went to the Rev James Newman. But he was a sick man and on 19 Feb 1872, Kilvert wrote: *He ought never to have been appointed by the Bishop, and he ought never to have accepted the living.*

Due to his illness Newman was often absent from meetings, yet during his his time the church was restored, All Saint's parish established and two new Church Schools built.

Samuel Alford the curate of Glasbury in Kilvert's time, lived with his eight children in the Vicarage which was a medieval building erected by monks from Gloucester. It stands between the site of the old church and Glasbury House. Kilvert describes it as a damp, desolate house and unhealthy being too close to the river. Alford stayed there for 23 years and died in office. He is remembered in Glasbury Church by the window over the chancel arch and a brass plaque by the lectern.

St Peter's Church, Glasbury, was built in 1837

Old painting of the *Three Cocks* Inn

Continue along the A438 to reach **Three Cocks** which was once an important railway junction of the Hereford, Hay & Brecon Railway with the Mid Wales Railway which became the Cambrian Railway in about 1890. The Hereford to Brecon line had been started as a private enterprise by the energetic promoter and builder of railways, Thomas Savin. It opened in 1864 but was leased in 1874 by the Midland Railway, with the idea of linking their main line routes with Swansea. The GWR eventually took over the line. The site of the station is now a Garden Centre. Also of interest to the present day traveller is the 17th century *Three Cocks* Inn, an ancient L-shaped building on the left side of the road and once an important stage on the old coach road. The *Three Cocks* sign dates from the battles of Potiers and Crécy when a descendant of one of the Welsh rulers fought under Edward III. His service was rewarded by the King with a coat of arms - three cocks on a silver shield. This later became the arms of the Williams family of Gwernyfed.

Take the next turning on the right (A4079) and follow this road through Llyswen and then past a turning which leads into the village of Boughrood (pronounced Bockrood). Shortly on the right will be seen the entrance drive to Llangoed Hall, a very fine building, restored in recent years by Sir Bernard Ashley and now a four star hotel.

After a few miles you will pass through **Erwood** which was called Y Rhyd in Welsh, meaning 'The Ford'. It was here that the Welsh drovers, after crossing the Cambrian Mountains, forded the Wye, driving their cattle to the English markets. By Kilvert's time the ford had been replaced by a ferry while today one crosses the river on a bridge.

Take the next turning on the right, about a mile beyond Erwood (signposted Aberedw and Painscastle) to cross the Wye. On joining the B4567, turn left to shortly reach the old Erwood Railway Station, which is now a craft centre, established in 1984 by Alan and Erika Cunningham. It is a picturesque spot with refreshments, picnic area, toilets etc available. In addition it is situated on the Wye Valley Walk and National Cycle Route 8. The premises is open seven days a week from mid-February to the end of December 9am-6pm in the spring and summer, and 10am-5pm in the autumn and winter (Tel: 01982 560674).

A couple of miles to the east of here is the deep gorge of the Bach-howey containing a a location known as Craig Pwll Du (The Rock of the Black Pool) and a very inaccessible waterfall. Kilvert made two visits there, once with his friend Hopwell Morrell of Cae Mawr and later in the company of an old mole catcher.

> *Far below us, as we stood on the cliffs, a round green knoll rose between the jaws of the narrow deep ravine. Then we began to descend the cliffs, while louder and louder came the thunder of the falls, until at last we reached the green knoll. 'Here', said the mole-catcher, 'stood the tower of a Welsh robber chieftain, who ravaged the country and carried off captives to his strong-hold; if they were not ransomed, he hurled them from the top of the crag into the Black Pool far below'.*
>
> *We climbed down the zig zag path, catching for support at the hazel bushes which fringed it; the thunder had become almost deafening but the fall itself was still hidden behind the jutting angle of a monstrous black rock, which hung frowning over the rushing stream, and seemed almost abruptly to close the gorge. At last we came within sight of the fall. Through a narrow rift in the huge black rocks burst a tumultuous mass of snowy foam that plunged forty feet into the black boiling pool below, with a thunderous roar that made the cliffs tremble. Rising sheer from the water's edge, the cliffs stood up black and towering round the pool, while the rocks reeked and*

*dripped continually with the spray. The tops of the cliffs were fringed with brushwood and low trees, and a gleam from the setting sun gilded the rocks at the mouth of the chasm, making the gloom within yet more intense. There was a tradition that the Black Pool had never been fathomed, although the mole-catcher had been present when an attempt was made. A hundred-pound weight was tied to the knotted bellropes of Trewerne church and lowered down, but even this length of rope could not reach the bottom. I shall not easily forget the beauty of the scene as we climbed up again from the deep ravine. From a sky of rose and gold the sun was sinking behind the mountains of Carmarthenshire, while the Black Mountains of Breconshire were bathed in a glow which made them look like a mass of pink granite. Gradually the light changed from rose and lilac to violet, then to a deep purple, until at last all was grey, and the horizon settled into a clear low splendour that heralded a frost.*

**WARNING: This cataract is difficult and dangerous in its approach. It now requires the use of a rope to make the descent and therefore no description of the route to reach it is given in this book.**

Continue along the B4567, passing below the **Aberedw Rocks** which Kilvert found so impressive:

*I never had a lovelier journey up the lovely valley of the Wye. A tender beautiful haze veiled the distant hills and woods with a gauze of blue and silver and pearl. It was a dream of intoxicating beauty. I saw all the familiar sights, the broad river reach at Boughrood flashing round the great curve in the sunlight over its hundred steps and rock ledges, the luxuriant woods which fringe the gleaming river lit up here and there by the golden flame of a solitary ash, the castled rock-towers and battlements and bastions of the rocks of Aberedw, the famous rocky wooded gorge through the depths of which the narrow mountain stream of the Edw rushed foaming to its Aber to meet the Wye ...*

Ahead soon will be seen a range of hills called the Carneddau (not to be confused with 3,000 feet mountains of the same name in North Wales). On reaching a junction turn left onto the A481. At the next junction turn left again to follow theA483. To visit **Builth Wells** turn left at a roundabout which is reached shortly.

Known by the Romans as Bulloeum, this little market town stands at the confluence of the River Wye and the River Irfon. It was known by the Welsh as Llanfair-ym-Muallt (The Church of St Mary in the cow pasture) and was granted a Charter by Edward I in 1278. In 1691 most of the town was destroyed by fire and today by far the oldest structure is the tower of **St Mary's Church**. Builth in the 19th century became famous for its mineral waters and the suffix Wells was added to the name. There are two groups of chalybeate springs, the Park Wells and the Glanne Wells which are both situated outside the town. The graceful bridge of six arches spanning the Wye was built in 1760.

Kilvert made his first visit to Builth Wells on May 29th, 1865 and enthused about *a glamour and enchantment about the first view of the shining slate roofs of Builth and the bridge and the winding reaches of the broad and shining river.*

From the roundabout mentioned above, follow the A470 past the Royal Welsh Showground at Llanelwedd (annual show usually held in the third week of July) and continue in the direction of Rhyader (13 miles). The next turning on the left is of interest in the fact that it leads down to 'Builth Road Railway Station'. In Kilvert's time there was also an important station known as Llechryd for it was the junction of two lines. The old Mid Wales Railway on which he frequently travelled to reach Newbridge, Rhyader and St Harmons is now no longer in existence, but the other line known as the 'Heart of Wales Railway', running between Swansea and Shrewsbury is still in use. When the Mid Wales Railway was being constructed, part of Aberedw Castle was destroyed, including one of the circular towers on its south side and the stone used to build a wall enclosing the yard at Builth Road Station.

Continue along the A470 to reach **Newbridge-on-Wye** (GR 016581), once famous for its horse fairs. Park on the left near the entrance to the churchyard. This village was previously known as Pontnewydd (Newbridge) and is named after a bridge erected here in 1679 to replace an earlier one mentioned by Leland in the 1530s. The 17th century bridge was replaced in 1835 by a wooden bridge of seven arches and this in turn was replaced in 1911 by one of masonry and ferro-concrete.

The church dedicated to All Saints was designed by S.W. Williams of Rhyader and built at the expense of George Stavin Venables QC, brother of the Vicar of Clyro, at a cost of £4,600.

All Saints Church Newbridge-on-Wye

The figures of Aaron, Moses and Joshua in the west window are said to bear the faces of the three Venables brothers; Richard Lister, George Stovin and Joseph Henry. There is a wall memorial on the south wall commemorating Richard and Agnes Minna Venables. The latter was responsible for carving the fine oak choir stall panels and it is significant that Kilvert speaks of her woodcarving skills in his *Diary*. This good lady is also commemorated by the beautiful marble mosaic floor in the sanctuary which was laid in her memory in 1900.

Kilvert frequently visited the Venables family at Llysdinam, travelling there by train from Hay and he sometimes preached in the temporary iron church at Llysdinam which was in use before the parish church of Newbridge was built in 1883.

> *I went to Llysdinam by 1.18 train, and my spirits rose as we passed up the beautiful valley amongst the old familiar scenes. The morning had been grey and overcast, but before we reached Erwood there came a sunburst and the gleam, swiftly broadening as the clouds scattered, stole over the green hillsides and the faint blue far-off mountains till the glory spread over the land of Llewellyn and the river sparkled down to the ford of Cavan Twm Bach and the enchanted valley lay smiling in all its loveliness.*

*As we glided up the valley, sweeping round bend after bend we saw new prospects and beauties still unfolding and opening before us, distant azure mountains, green sunny bursts and dark blue wooded hollows of the nearer hills with gentle dips and dimpling swells on the hillsides softly bosoming. Then suddenly came a vivid flash, dazzling with a blaze of diamond sparks thrown off as if by a firework, on the stream suddenly caught and tangled amongst broken rocks, swept roaring in a sheet of white foam through the narrowing channel, or with a stately and gracious bend the river broadened, peaceful and calm, to majestic reach, long and silver shining, veiled here and there by fringing, overhanging woods and broken by the larch spires dawning a thickening green.*

**Llysdinam Hall** is situated on high ground overlooking Newbridge-on-Wye. It is an impressive mansion surrounded by well kept gardens and ornamental grounds. Originally it was built by Thomas Huet, Precentor of St David's and Rector of Cefnllys and Disserth. He died in 1591 and was buried at Llanavan Church about 4 miles away. In about 1830 Llysdinam became the family home of Richard Venables, Archdeacon of Carmarthen, Vicar of Clyro, Nantmel and Llanyre.

Richard Venables had two sons, and it was the eldest, Richard Lister Venables who took over as Vicar of Clyro parish in 1847, after serving for some years as his father's curate. The second son was George Stavin who became a prominent barrister and as a poet he was able to boast that he had known Tennyson at Cambridge.

In 1871 Kilvert mentions that the house was being enlarged, no doubt ready for the resignation of Rev Venables from the parish of Clyro when he would take up permanent residence at Llysdinam. He was JP for the counties of Radnor, Brecknock and Hereford as well as being for some time vicar of Clyro. In 1834 he had married Mary Augusta Dalrymple, daughter of General Poltoratzky of Russia. She died in 1865 and two years later he married Agnes Minna, youngest daughter of Henry Shepherd Pearson, by whom he had one son (who died in 1876) and two daughters, Katharine Minna and Caroline Emily. His wife, Agnes was the niece of Vice-Admiral Lord Lyons, who as Commander of the Mediterranean Fleet, had his headquarters in Malta. When Richard Lister Venables died on Jan 3rd 1894, he was succeeded in the estate by Katharine Minna. In 1893 she married Sir Charles Dilwyn Llewelyn who by Royal Licence changed his surname to Dilwyn Venables Llewelyn.

Llysdinam Hall is situated on high ground overlooking Newbridge-on-Wye

The Rev Lister Venables actually outdid Kilvert by writing 79 volumes of diaries, which came to light in 1971 and are preserved at the National Library in Aberystwyth. When he died he was buried in the churchyard of All Saints, Newbridge-on-Wye.

Llysdinam Hall was largely rebuilt in 1936 and from 1970, the Department of Applied Biology of the University of Wales Institute of Science & Technology, UWIST, has had a Field Study Centre on the Llysdinam Estate of the Venables Llewelyn family. It serves as a base for research into the environment of mid-Wales and students come here from schools, colleges and universities throughout Britain for residential field courses.

It is worth making a short detour from Newbridge-on-Wye to visit **Disserth Church**. Turn right in front of the *New Inn* (on B4358) and then take the next turning on the right (signposted Disserth 1 mile). Just after crossing the River Ithon turn right and drive down to Disserth Church ( GR 035583 ). There is parking available in front of the entrance to the churchyard. The name Disserth comes from the Latin *disertum* meaning hermitage or refuge and the church may well be built on the site of St Cewydd's simple cell or hermitage beside the river Ithon.

It is a lovely old church with a squat castellated tower, containing the oldest bell in Radnorshire, dating from 1300, an ancient font, square pews bearing the names of their occupiers as far back as 1666, and a 17th century three-decker pulpit. Kilvert, writing on the 14th July, 1871, mentioned how Old Mr Thomas the Vicar of Disserth... *would get up in the pulpit without an idea about what he was going to say, and would begin thus 'Ha, yes here we are. And it is a fine day. I congratulate you on the fine day, and glad to see so many of you here. Yes indeed. Ha, yes, very well. Now then I shall take for my text so and so. Yes, let me see. You are all sinners and so am I. Yes indeed.'*

Return to Newbridge-on-Wye and turn right on the A470 which is now followed to **Rhyader**. Situated beside a ford of the Wye, 700 feet above sea-level, Rhyader has always been an important stopping point for travellers en route for Aberystwyth or journeying between South and North Wales.

The town owes its Welsh name of Rhaidr Gwy (Cataract on the Wye) to a series of small falls which were largely destroyed in 1780 when the channel was widened and rocks removed to build the stone bridge carrying the main road over the river. This was the mail coach route to Aberystwyth which was then growing in popularity.

For several centuries the town was dominated by a castle standing on a hillock overlooking the Wye, but today hardly a trace of it remains. It was built in about 1178 by Rhys ap Gruffydd, Prince of South Wales, but captured by the Mortimers of Wigmore soon after his death in 1197. Llywelyn the Great burned it down in 1215 and it was never rebuilt.

In 1878 Kilvert visited the town and watched a large party of Rebeccaites...*out spearing salmon below Rhyader Bridge...a most picturesque sight*.

The original Rebeccaites were those who violently opposed the turnpike system and took their name from Genesis where Rebecca's descendants 'will possess the gates of them that hate them.' Disguised as women they attacked and burned the gates.

Salmon poachers took advantage of the situation and adopted the name and disguise as Rebecca and her Daughters. Working at night in gangs, armed with spears and carrying torches, they were responsible for the destruction of vast quantities of salmon in the upper reaches of the Wye and in the Irthon Valley. Their actions were directed at the unpopular Fishery Laws and took place until long after the genuine Rebecca Riots had died down. One of the earliest of the Rebecca Fishery Riots was in 1856, but they were at their worst between 1878 and 1882, when the police and water bailiffs had many clashes between gangs of up to a hundred men, all disguised, and armed with guns and bludgeons.

Disserth Church stands on an ancient site beside the River Ithon

This engraving shows the waterfall on the Wye at Rhyader, where in 1878, Kilvert observed a gang of salmon poachers dressed in the style of the Rebecca rioters

After exploring Rhyader, turn right past the Leisure Centre to follow the B4518 (signposted St Harmons). The road climbs steadily and as you come over a rise you will look down on the sleepy village of **St Harmons**. Across to the left can be seen a recently established windfarm. Kilvert no doubt would have been appalled to see such an intrusion in his beloved Radnorshire countryside!

A sign announces that you are entering SAINT HARMONS and the little church will be found on the right (GR 989228). Dedicated to St Garmon it stands on a mound within a circular churchyard which is an indication that it is an ancient foundation. St Garmon is said to have come here in the fifth century and prayed with his clergy against the sins of Vortigern.

Giraldus Cambrensis paid a visit to the church in 1188 and noted that here was preserved the sacred staff of St Curig. Carved on all sides with silver and gold it was shaped in the form of a cross and was credited with healing powers. Sufferers from glandular diseases who approached the staff in the proper spirit and at the same time presented some money to the church, apparently found it provided an unfailing cure for their particular complaints.

The relic was probably confiscated at the time of the Dissolution of the Monasteries and stripped of its casing of gold and silver. But there is also a belief that it was hidden in some secret place and is yet to be found.

St Harmon's Church, where Kilvert served as Vicar for just under a year in 1878

In 1821 the church was rebuilt, having previously been described by a churchwarden as 'a piece of architecture so deformed and so ill-contrived yet very expensive to keep in repair and is chiefly resorted unto by disturbers of divine worship.'

The new church was quaint with a double-decker pulpit and box-shaped pews. Each of these pews had the name of a St Harmon farmer painted on its door, for when this church was built many farmers bought a 'seat' by funding the cost of a pew. The custom was, that when one of the farmers died, or moved to another holding, the pew became the property of his successor.

This system of allocating pews or seats to houses was by no means peculiar to Radnorshire, but it may have lingered longer in this county than elsewhere. The 'great house' of the parish usually had a special pew of its own, rather larger than the rest, and sometimes with higher sides which could be curtained, so that long sermons could be endured with some degree of comfort and repose.

The living of St Harmons became vacant on the death of the Rev Bowen Evans in April 1876 and was worth £161 per annum (raised to £177 by 1877) but at that time there was no vicarage. It was Kilvert's old vicar at Clyro, the Rev R.L. Venables who suggested that he should consider applying for the living of St Harmons.

> *This morning a letter came from Mr Venables saying that Archdeacon De Winton, the Archdeacon of Brecon, had written to him to ask if I would entertain the idea of going to St Harmon's should the Bishop of St David's offer me the Living. The old Vicar, Bowen Evans, is just dead. I wrote to the Archdeacon to ask for a few days' grace till I go to St Harmons from Llysdinam and see the place. I think I would accept the living. I am not sure that I should be justified in refusing it, as it will be worth between £300 and £400 a year when the lease on one or two old lives falls in....*

When Kilvert first visited St Harmons on 4th May, 1876, he sat in the churchyard eating his sandwiches, the silence only broken by the sound of the sheep and the cry of a cuckoo, but he described the church as being *simply hideous*.

> *Soon after leaving Rhyader the railway leaves the valley of the Wye and enters the sweet vale of Marteg by a wild and narrow*

*gorge which soon opens, broadens and settles down into a winding valley shut in by gentle hills about which are dotted lone white cottages and farms. The little by-station of St Harmon's is kept by a handsome, pleasant-faced woman, very stout, who lives in a cottage on the line. The Church stands close to the station on a little mount half veiled by a clump of trees. It was built in the Dark Ages of fifty years ago and was simply hideous. But ugly as it appeared externally the interior was worse and my heart sank within me like a stone as I entered the door. A bare cold squalid interior and high ugly square boxes for seats, a three-decker pulpit and desk, no stove, a flimsy altar rail, a ragged faded altar cloth, a singing gallery with a broken organ, a dark little box for a vestry and a roof in bad repair, admitting the rain. Such was St Harmon's Church as I first saw it.*

On the 11th June, 1878 Kilvert wrote in his diary: *This morning came a letter from the Bishop of St David's offering me the Vicarage of St Harmon's. I wrote and accepted it.*

Having taken such a dislike to the church on his initial visit, it is surprising that Kilvert decided to apply for the position as vicar. But he perhaps reluctantly did so because he wanted to progress his career.

Kilvert was appointed Vicar on 21 July 1876 but was unable to occupy the vicarage because someone else was living there. So he took lodgings at Old Bank House (now demolished), opposite the *Old Crown* Inn at Rhyader, 4 miles outside his parish. He travelled to perform his duties at the church by train (to the halt just above the church) or by carriage and he also sometimes walked, particularly on Sundays.

Of interest in the church is the Litany Desk which in memory of Francis Kilvert, was given to St Harmons in 1950 with money raised by parishioners and The Kilvert Society. A red granite memorial in the churchyard commemorates Sarah Jones 'Stationmistress for 36 years', She was the *handsome pleasant-faced woman, very stout* mentioned by Kilvert in his *Diary* on 4 May 1876.

There is a pub in the village called *The Sun* and it was here that Kilvert toasted the newly-married David Powell and Maggie Jones on 26 April 1878. Opposite the inn is Wesley Place, the former Methodist Chapel which held services in Welsh until 1870. It closed in the early 1970s.

Unfortunately there is a missing period in the *Diary* for the time that Kilvert spent at St Harmons. Between June 1876 and December 1877 there is a long gap and it is believed that these entries were destroyed by Kilvert's widow after his death. He was obviously not happy at St Harmons for he resigned and left within a year even though no one at the time had been appointed to replace him. Possibly he considered St Harmons an unsuitable place to bring a wife, particularly without a proper home to offer her.

On your return journey down the Wye Valley you may be interested in diverting from Builth Wells to visit **Llanlleonfel Church** which Kilvert described in August 1873.

After crossing the bridge over the Wye, turn right into the main street of Builth Wells and follow the A483 out of town to pass through Cilmery. Here on the left you will see a tall monolith of Caernarvonshire granite marking the place where Llywelyn ap Gruffudd, the grandson of Llywelyn ap Iorwerth was murdered in 1282. He also became known as Llywelyn ein Llyw Olaf - 'Llywelyn our Last Leader' - the last native Prince of Wales.

Memorial to Llywelyn ap Gruffudd - the last native Prince of Wales

Llanleonfel Church was in ruins when Kilvert visited it in 1873

Drive on beside the Heart of Wales Railway line, through Garth and across the river Dulas to reach **Llanlleonfel**. Kilvert came here on 6th August, 1873, when staying with the Venables family at Llysdinam and at that time this church was in ruins. There was no glass in the windows and it was bare inside apart from an old pulpit.

> *The ruined Church tottered lone upon a hill in desolate silence. The old tombstones stood knee-deep in the long coarse grass and white and purple flowers nodded over the graves. The door stood open and I went in. The window frames and seats were gone. Nothing was left but the high painted deal pulpit bearing the sacred monogram in yellow letters. Some old memorial tablets bearing Latin inscriptions in remembrance of Marmaduke Gwynne and his family were affixed to the East Wall. The place was utterly deserted, there was not a sound. But through the ruined windows I could see the white tents of the flower show in the valley beneath. I ascended the tall rickety pulpit and several white owls disturbed from their day sleep floated silently under a crazy Rood Loft on their broad downy wings and sauntered sailing without a sound through the frameless east and west windows to take refuge with a graceful sweep of their broad white pinions in the ancient yew that kept watch over the Church. It was a place for owls to dwell in and for satyrs to dance in.*

Three years after Kilvert's visit, Llanlleonfel Church was rebuilt at a cost of £900. The Vicar of Llanlleonfel and Eglwys Oen Duw at this time was the Rev Montague Earle Welby, who had served as a locum to Mr Venables during his holiday in May 1870 and was thus known to Kilvert.

Theophilus Jones in *A History of Brecknock* suggests the origin of the name of this church may have been 'Llan Lleon Voel' - 'Church upon the bare moor'. It is certainly situated in a prominent position on a small rise above a branch of the old Roman road connecting Neath and Chester. A simple church may have existed here in the Dark Ages but the present building was erected in the 19th century.

It is of interest that the well known hymn writer, Charles Wesley was married here in 1749 to Sally Gwynne, daughter of Marmaduke Gwynne who lived at Garth House about half-a-mile away. A plaque commemorating this marriage can be seen on the north wall of the church.

# CAR TOUR TO BREDWARDINE

## *The Final Journey*

37 ½ miles (60 km)

From Clyro follow the A438 through Bronydd (referred to by Kilvert as Bronith) and past the *Rhydspence Inn* to reach Whitney-on-Wye. The tower of the church will soon be seen on the left. Turn left (signposted Whitney Church) and park near the lychgate (GR 268475).

Whitney is derived from Witeni or Witena, which in Saxon means 'a clear water stream with boggy islands'. It is given a mention in *Domesday Book* which records that 'The King holds Witeni in Elsedna hundred.'

The name has also been translated as 'Hwita's island' and this may have been the island in the River Wye about a quarter of a mile SE of the church. There was once a Norman castle at Whitney, but that was washed away in a flood and is now only visible as a sandspit (GR 272465).

In the Middle Ages the Whitney family who held this place, traced their descent from Thurston the Fleming, a companion of Duke William, who received the Wigmore district after the Conquest and married Agnes, the only child of Aluned de Merleburgh. Thurston was also given Whitney and his son took the surname de Whitney.

A Sir Robert de Whitney in 1368 was chosen to accompany the Duke of Clarence with two hundred knights and gentlemen to Milan to marry Violante Visconti, daughter of the Duke of Milan. In 1377 he was Sheriff of the county, and represented it several times in Parliament. He was Richard II's friend, but deserted him for Henry Bolingbroke and fell against Owain Glyndwr in 1401, when his castle of Whitney was taken and burnt. His son Sir Robert, was compensated by the king, and was at Agincourt with Henry V. The original church was swept away in the great flood of 1735, when the Wye took a new course, and its site is to be found a little below where the old Court stood.

It is known from the Domesday Book that there was a church or private chapel at Whitney in 1160-70, held with Whitney lands, by the Baskerville family. The earliest known date for a Rector was an appointment in 1285, when the Whitney family appear as patrons.

Dedicated to St Peter and St Paul, the present **Whitney Church**, was erected on a safer site in 1735 and was financed by the the Squire, Mr Wardour of Old Whitney Court. He was descended from the Whitney family and inherited estates which go back to the 13th century. The church was considerably restored with some alterations in 1904 and the tower was originally taller with a higher spire. Inside the church is a Norman font and some of the pews and panelling which were salvaged from the old church.

Also of interest is the window with figures of St George and the Madonna which was given in 1908 in memory of Major Frederick Napleton Dew, who had served in the Indian Mutiny and the Crimean War. Another window depicting Peter and Paul was set up to mark the jubilee of his relation, the rector Henry Dew. When the latter died he had served here for fifty-eight years and in 1903 a new lychgate was built as a tribute to his long ministry. Also a tablet was set up to commemorate John Turner, who served him as parish clerk for over half a century.

In 1909 the 17th century pulpit and lectern were put in as a memorial to the Reverend Henry Dew, who was descended from the Wardour and Whitney family. The reredos over the altar is an overmantel from the 17th century Whitney Court (long destroyed), placed there to also mark Henry Dew's long incumbency.

Henry Dew lived with his family in Whitney Rectory, to which William Wordsworth was once a visitor, taking tea with the Rector on the terrace. He was in the locality visiting Miss Hutchinson, his wife's niece who was living at Stow Farm. Kilvert must have been very impressed by the fact that Wordsworth had visited the Dews for he was much influenced by the work of this well known Lakeland poet. In turn, Wordsworth was delighted with the scenery in the upper Wye Valley for according to Richard Venables he had commented that the river Wye above Hay offered the finest landscape in South Britain.

> *At noon got out my old Swiss haversack, crammed night necessaries into it, made a brown paper parcel of my dress coat, and strapping all together started after luncheon for Whitney Rectory, walking with my pack slung over my shoulders by the fields to Hay to catch the 1.50 train.*
>
> *At Whitney I walked down to the Rectory by the private path through the shrubbery. I went up the meadow to the Stow and found that Dewing had just gone out. However he had seen me coming and had left a message with a servant to ask me to wait and he would be in in a few minutes. I waited in the drawing room. The last time I was in that room was when Mr Venables and I rode to call upon the Dewings just after their marriage. And now she was dead. How well I remember the bride cake and wine on the table and she sitting in the window looking so well, so radiant and happy.*
>
> *The lilies of the valley that were planted by Miss Dew close by the front door in the little flower border to welcome the*

The Church of St Peter and St Paul, Whitney-on-Wye

The lychgate at Whitney church was built in 1903
as a tribute to the 58 year ministry of Henry Dew

*young bride on the first coming home, after her marriage on the 14th May, are now just coming up. So early dead, not 23, and to the poor bereaved husband after the short gleam of happiness all seems like a dream. Her pretty portrait still on the dining room mantlepiece. In the dining room on the bookshelves stood two cases of stuffed birds, one case of gulls and petrels, all the sea-birds from Plymouth. The other was a case of country birds, a cuckoo, jay, yappingdale, starling, blackbird and thrush, all nicely set up by her brother Mr Hinckstone. After waiting and waiting I went out into the garden and strolled about the sunny lawn where a slight shower from a black cloud had beaded the grass with bright drops. Presently I saw Miss Dew in her black dress coming slowly up the green meadow. I thought of William Wordsworth the poet who often used to come and stay at this house with blind Mr Monkhouse who had nearly all his poems off by heart. Miss Dew came in by the wicket gate leading from the garden into the meadow and stayed some time telling me about Mr Dewing.*

The Rev Henry Dew (brother of Tomkyns Dew, who lived at Whitney Court) was Rector of Whitney-on-Wye between 1843 and 1901. Henry and his wife Mary had ten children.

## Car Tour to Bredwardine

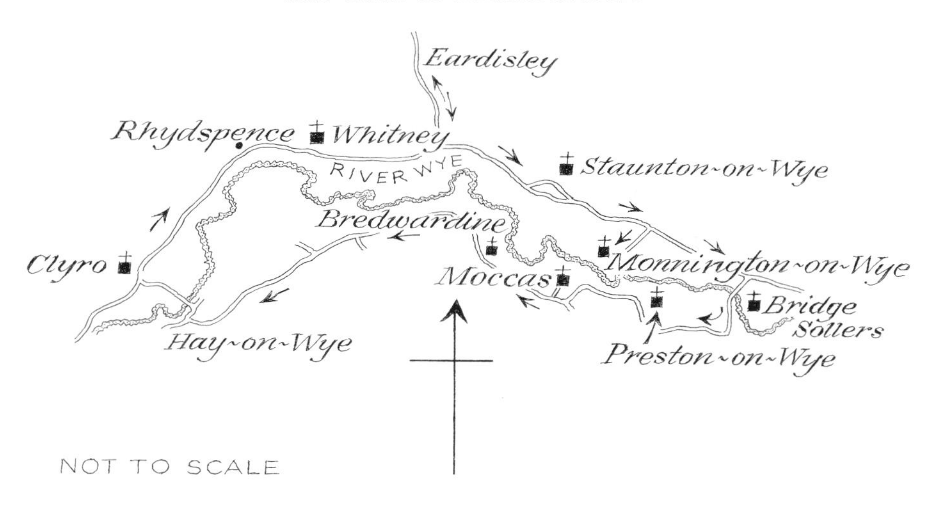

This stained glasss window at Whitney Church, depicting St Peter and St Paul was installed to mark the jubilee of the rector Henry Dew

*One of the dear old bright happy mornings which seem peculiar and sacred to Whitney Rectory. The sun shone brightly at the southern window bowered in roses and beautiful creeping plants and the birds chirped and sang in their bowers and I opened my eyes on the old familiar view as I looked up the valley of the Wye to the heights of Clyro Hill. Muirbach Hill dawned a soft azure through the tender morning mists. Pretty Louisa Dew bounded up the stairs to meet me with a bright rosy morning face and a lovely kiss, when she heard me leave my room. She will be a noble-looking girl one day and will make somebody's heart ache. She is a very fine girl for her age now and as wild as a hawk but as good as gold, in spite of her dancing spirits. After breakfast a ramble in the garden to see the fruit trees. A white nectarine was in a blaze of purple blossom.*

Louisa Dew (b.1865) was the youngest of the Dew's ten children who are all mentioned in the *Diary*: Emily (b. 1846), Jane Beatrice (b.1848), Henry Monkhouse (b.1850), Arthur Tomkyns (b.1853), Armine (b.1854), Helen Francis (b.1856), Edward (b.1859), Alice Horrocks (b.1860) and Walter (b.1864).

Henry and Mary Dew and several of the family, including his brother Tomkyns lie buried in the family vault in the north east corner of Whitney Churchyard. Tomkyns Dew was a magistrate and landowner (aged 53 in 1870) who lived at Whitney Court, which was not the present house which stands on the hill but a building which overlooked the river and has since been demolished.

Whitney Court was built in the early 1900s to replace the original house which was near the river and whose foundations were damaged by a flood.

*...as I walked down to the Church I heard the tones of the harmonium and the chanting. Henry Dew read the service and a Harvest sermon. After Church the whole parish, men, women and children, dined in the Rectory yard under a penthouse of beams, and tarpaulin, nearly 200 people. After dinner all the men played or rather kicked football at each other...it grew dark, when the game ended in a general royal scuffle and scrummage.*

The rectory at Whitney-on-Wye

*After breakfast I walked with Jane and Helen Dew for a charming walk.*

*We walked along Wordsworth's Terrace where he was taken once to see the view. He was staying at the Stow Farm at the time with his friend and relation, blind Mr Monkhouse. It was Sunday and the poet had been at Whitney Church in the morning and came up to the Rectory for luncheon. Henry Dew took him the same walk along the side of the hill, which is now called 'Wordsworth's Terrace', and when the great poet saw the river below winding down through the beautiful valley and the hill ranges rising one above another and the blue mountains behind crowning the whole, Clifford, Castleton Hill and the Wye, he was enraptured and said that though he had travelled through many countries he had never looked upon a more beautiful scene.*

This wooden footbridge can be seen just above the church. It spans the Hereford, Hay and Brecon Railway near the site of Whitney Station, to which Kilvert often travelled when visiting the Dew family at Whitney Rectory. To make this 4 mile journey by train, Kilvert had to first walk over a mile to Hay Station, but it meant that the journey was shortened by about half-an-hour.

There is a turning area provided above the lychgate where the road bends to the right. Return to the main road and turn left, to continue through Winforton, which is mentioned in *Domesday Book* as Widforstone, 'the village on the wide fording place'. The next village reached is Willersley which is called Willadeslege in the *Domesday Book*. On reaching a road junction turn left along the A4111 to reach **Eardisley** (derived from the Anglo Saxon Aegheard's leah). This attractive Herefordshire village is rich in timber-fronted houses. A lane on the left, opposite the village primary school provides access to Eardisley Church.

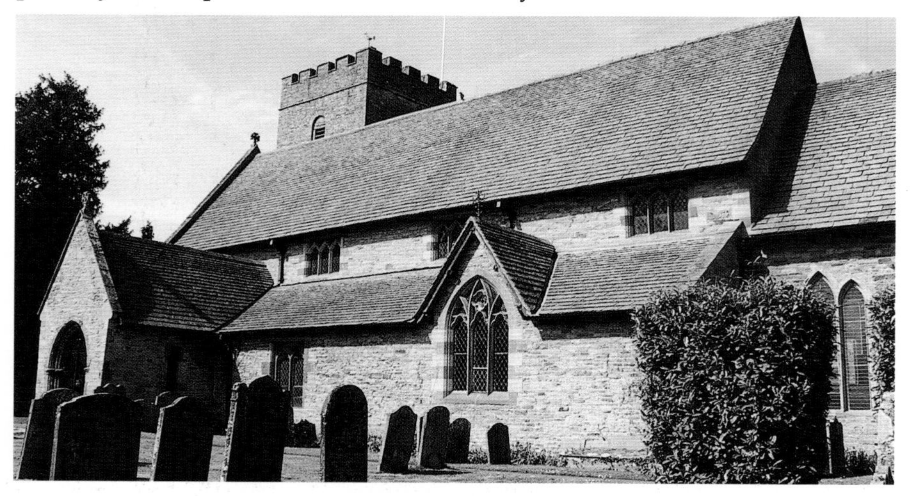

The Norman church at Eardisley

The church of **St Mary Magdalene** is unusually large with much Norman and Decorated work. But of very special interest is the font which has carvings on every inch of its surface and even the pedestal is covered with rich interlacing. The carvings around the bowl show in savage and vivid detail how the Welsh fought to hold back the invaders of their land. One section shows a warrior with raised sword just about to decapitate his adversary, but the man has been a little quicker, thrusting his spear through the leg of the swordsman. Another carving on the bowl shows Christ rescuing St Peter from a roaring lion, while St John stands calmly reading a book, which may well be the Holy Scriptures.

This beautiful font is a fine example of early medieval art and it was carved by a school of Celtic-Norman artisans who travelled throughout Herefordshire to decorate the blank stonework of many ecclesiastical buildings. Their finest work can be seen at Kilpeck Church between Abergavenny and Hereford.

This beautiful Norman font at Eardisley Church has been intricately carved by 12th century craftsmen

An oak tablet in the church gives a list of rectors from 1280, including Nicholas Hinton, who 'obtained permission in 1348 to go on a pilgrimage to the Holy Sepulchre.' Also featured is Samuel Hall, who came here in 1673 and ministered for 54 years.

A stone near the tower commemorates Thomas Bevan, Blacksmith, who died in 1744:-

My sledge and hammer lie declin'd
My bellows have quite lost their wind
My fires extinct, my forge decay'd
My vices in the dust all lay'd
My coals spent, my iron gone
My nails are drove, my work is done
My fire-dry'd corpse lies here at rest
My soul, smoak like is soaring to be blest.

The *Tram Inn* is a reminder of a horsedrawn tramway
which once linked Brecon with Kington

Upper House Farm on the outskirts of Eardisley dates back to the 14th century

The great Wellingtonia tree which towers above the north side of the churchyard was grown from seed brought back from the Yosemite Valley, USA, by the Rev Samuel Palmer, who was the Rector of Eardisley and fond of travelling abroad. It was this reverend gentleman who suggested to Kilvert at a garden party in June 1878 that he should take up the Chaplaincy of Cannes for it would be good for his health. But Kilvert turned down the offer.

Near the churchyard, a large mound, with a triple moat is the site of a fortified castle mentioned in *Domesday*. Constructed by Roger de Lacey soon after the Conquest this fortress subsequently became the home of the Baskervilles who were Lords of the Manor of Eardisley for over 400 years.

Early in the 12th century Ralph de Baskerville became involved in a land dispute with his new father-in-law, Lord Drogo of Clifford. He challenged Lord Drogo to mortal combat to settle matters. The fight took place at Whitecross, Hereford. Ralph won and his father-in-law died of his wounds. He later sought pardon from the Pope and eventually became a monk at Gloucester where he died in 1141.

The hated Bishop of Hereford Peter d' Aquablanca was held prisoner in Eardisley Castle in 1262 until his death a year later. He had been arrested at his altar in Hereford Cathedral, his priests slain and his treasure seized.

The last of the Baskervilles was Benhail who was living here in comparative poverty in 1670. During the Civil War the end of the castle came when Cromwell and Royalist forces seem to have torn the building down between them and a Georgian building known as Castle Farm now stands on its site.

The *Tram Inn* is named after a horse-drawn tramway which connected Brecon with Kington and served Eardisley well before the coming of the steam railway. Trams of coal were hauled by horses until 1864 when the railway came, utilising much of the old track. The railway closed in 1962.

On the outskirts of the village is Upper House Farm, parts of which date from the 14th century and additions were made in the 16th century. In a projecting gable is the Coffin Window belonging to the Coffin Room. It lights a small attic room shaped like a coffin. This is where the monks who originally lived in the house were laid out when they died with a candle left burning in the window, so according to an old tradition the villagers seeing the light would kneel outside and pray for the dead man's soul to find rest.

It is claimed that Cromwell once lodged here when attacking Eardisley Castle. Nearby is a field known as Cannon Field where the Parliamentary forces forded a stream which fed the castle moat and dragged their heavy artillery across it.

Having explored Eardisley, return the way you have come to rejoin the A438 and turn left towards Hereford. After passing through Letton and past the *Swan Inn,* look out for a turning on the left to **Staunton-on-Wye** (easily missed, but if you miss the first turning there is a second one further on). As you drive through this village you will observe some interesting names such as 'Little London', 'World's End' and 'Duck Street'. The name Staunton was originally Standon and at the time of the Domesday Survey, the manor belonged to Roger de Laci of Weobley. At the far end of the village turn down a road to the right (signposted 'To the Church').

Staunton-on-Wye Church with its unusual pyramidal spire

**Staunton-on-Wye Church**, perched on a knoll above the road, has some Norman features and fine Jacobean panelling. The ancient church spire has been replaced by a lower one of pyramidal design. It was an old man of this village called James Meredith who told Kilvert in January, 1878, how he *was watching the oxen on old Christmas Eve and at 12 o' clock the oxen that were standing knelt down upon their knees and those that were lying down rose up on their knees and there they stayed kneeling and moaning, the tears running down their faces.*

Continue to meet the main road (A438) and turn left. On reaching the *Portway Inn* (on the left) turn right, with care, to follow the road directly opposite (to Monnington-on-Wye), passing between extensive apple orchards, owned by Bulmers Ltd. of Hereford, the world's largest cider making company, who purchased land here from the Cornewall family of Moccas in 1965.

(**NOTE: This lane is unsuitable for coaches and there is very limited parking by the church**).

Park on the grass verge, just before reaching the drive to Monnington Court. Follow a grass path on the left (part of the Wye Valley Walk) to a metal gate and then on to the lychgate.

At Monnington can be seen *the old slanting mouldering lych-gate, gabled on all sides*

Monnington Church was rebuilt (except the tower) in 1679 by Ulvedall and Mary Tomkyns of Monnington Court, who are commemorated by grave slabs in the chancel.

**Monnington Church** (GR 373433) and Monnington Court stand side by side and were built after the restoration of Charles II. Monnington, an Anglo-Saxon name means 'settlement of Manna's people' and today the hamlet consists of the 17th century Court, St Mary's Church and a few cottages. Two wealthy landowners, Ulvedall and Mary Tomkyns built the church in 1679. Their initials can be seen on the font and the whole building is a period piece with fine oak benches, like settles and 'twisted barley sugar shafts'. There is a fine carved coat of arms of Charles II and the font is dated 1680. The builders retained the 15th century church tower.

Kilvert's sister Thersie (Thermuthis) moved to Monnington-on-Wye from the City of Bath when her husband William Smith became the Rector here (from 1875-1889). They had four children, Hastings, Perceval, Florence and Essex (later Mrs Essex Hope). It was Perceval Smith who submitted the *Diary* for publication in the 1930s.

The family took up residence in the large brick built vicarage with extensive grounds that reached down to the mile long Walk of Scots Pines referred to by Kilvert as the 'Royal Walk'.

It is evident from his *Diary* entries that Kilvert took great pleasure in coming to Monnington-on-Wye, and found it a very peaceful place. On 23rd, April, 1876 he wrote:-

*I like a Sunday at Monnington, it is so calm and so serene. There is no hurry, no crowd, no confusion, no noise.*

*The silver birch droops and waves her long dusky tress as a maiden with delicate white limbs and slender arms and hands lets down her long hair and combs it to the curve of her beautiful knees shrinking from sight and hiding herself in the dusky cloud and twilight of her tresses rippling to her feet.*

*Then I love to walk up the great avenue, as up a vast and solemn Cathedral aisle, while the wind sighs through the branches of tall sombre Scotch firs overhead and makes mournful music as it breathes upon that natural Aeolian harp which is the organ in that Cathedral. The Choir is comprised of the wild birds and with their songs chimes in the flowing river as it rushes over the rocks and the voices of bells ringing for service from the hillsides around.*

*The three bells of Monnington begin to chime quickly from the Church Tower beyond the old grey mansion of the Glendowers. We stroll down the lane over the pitched pavement. Along the larches which line the old slanting mouldering lych-gate sit four or five boys. The bells stop, the clerk French appears standing bareheaded in the churchyard by the flat and broken gravestone of 'Owen Glendwrdwy divine', looking to see if anyone is coming to church. An old man and two or three women heave in sight coming along the high walk by the side of the low osier bed now gay with the golden clumps of marsh marigolds. The Priest's bell strikes up, we enter the church and robe in the vestry, the chief farmer (James of Monnington Court) comes in in his grey coat, followed by his wife. Thersie plays the harmonium and the service begins. I read prayers in the morning and William preached, a slight but masterly and impressive sermon.'*

Kilvert made the mistake of thinking that Owain Glyndwr was buried near the church porch:

> *Hard by the Church porch and on the western side of it I saw what I knew must be the grave of Owen Glendower. It is a flat stone of whitish grey shaped like a rude obelisk figure, sunk deep into the ground in the middle of an oblong patch of earth from which the turf has been pared away, and, alas, smashed into several fragments.*
>
> *And here in the little Herefordshire churchyard within hearing of the rushing of the Wye and close under the shadow of the old grey church the strong wild heart, still now, has rested by the ancient home and roof tree of his kindred since he fell asleep there more than four hundred years ago. It is a quiet peaceful spot.*

On another occasion Kilvert recorded how he was told (by Mr James):

> *... that in the great flood of February 6, 1852, he and the present Sir Gilbert Lewis of Harpton (then Rector of Monnington) had punted in a flat-bottomed boat across the Court garden, in at the Church door, up the Nave and into the Chancel. The flood that day rose as high in the Church as the seats of the benches.*

The Monnington Walk was described by Kilvert as 'a noble avenue of magnificent Scotch first bordering a green ride, stretching from Brobury Scar to Monnington Court...' These trees were planted by James Tomkyns, grandfather of Ulvedale Tomkyns to celebrate his election as MP for Leominster in 1623. Twenty years later he was hanged for raising a troop for the king against Parliament. The Monnington Walk is now part of the Wye Valley Walk and it is a 3 mile walk along this route to Bredwardine.

Return up the lane to reach the main road (A438), opposite the *Portway Inn* and turn right. The nearest crossing point on the Wye is at Bridge Sollers which is about 2 miles away. On reaching a crossroads turn right (signposted Madley and Preston-on-Wye) to pass **Bridge Sollers Church**, standing on a high bank, beside the road on the left. Dedicated to St Andrew, it was restored in 1889 at a cost of £500 raised by public subscription in memory of a late vicar, the Rev R. H. Williams. The chancel is 13th century, the aisle a century younger while the nave, its arcade, and the lower part of the tower are Norman. There are curious carvings on the imposts of the doorway. A dragon stares at you while two others are depicted emerging out of a man's head.

This location was called Brige (bridge) in the Domesday Survey and Sollers is a Norman family name, probably derived from Soliers, near Caen.

The road descends to a stone bridge, built in 1897, to replace a ferry. After just over a mile, turn right at a junction (signposted Preston-on-Wye). Drive through this village following the Moccas road. Just outside the village a road on the right leads down past a large pool which once adjoined a mill (burned down during the 2nd World War), to **Preston-on-Wye Church** (GR 383424) which has a large car park. The name Preston is from the Old English and means 'settlement of the priests'.

Preston-on-Wye Church

It is a spacious church, full of light from unstained windows set in the fine grey walls. It was largely built in the 19th century but has a Norman doorway and a window of that age in the opposite wall. The font bowl is a copy of Norman work set on the old base. When Kilvert visited this church, the Vicar told him that he intended *moving it up to the village green by the old tree where it will be more in the centre of the population*. However he did not carry out such a bold plan and instead the church was much restored (or destroyed !) by Nicholson in 1883.

Return to the Moccas road, turn right and about 200 yards before reaching the B4352, turn sharp right by a small lodge (not the first lodge that you pass). Drive through the gateway and through the pleasant parkland to shortly turn left along a broad track leading to a parking area in front of **Moccas Church** (GR 357434) which is dedicated to St Michael and All Angels.

The church of St Michael and All Angels at Moccas

Moccas, or Mochras ('the moor of pigs') as it was once called was the name of a district which extended down the Wye for some distance. In 1878 Kilvert wrote:

> *When Moccas Church was restored and reopened the Archdeacon preached in the afternoon and told the people that Moccas was so called from 'the badgers which came down the river to eat the fish'.*

Kilvert no doubt meant otters, and had in some strange way mixed up otters, badgers and pigs, for Moccas is so called from the swine (Welsh Moch) which used to feed on the acorns in the great oak forest.

Founded in the 6th century by St Dubricius, Moccas Church was rebuilt in stone by the Normans in the 12th century

The first church is said to have been founded here by St Dubricius in the latter half of the 5th century. It must have been a mud and wattle structure and was rebuilt in stone during the 12th century by the Normans.

> *Yesterday Bishop promised to meet me at noon to-day at Moccas Church and show me over it. As I crossed Moccas bridge I heard a chime of deep melodious voices and at the next lodge I came upon four men, wandering singers, with voices matched like bells, singing in harmony and exquisitely melodious, but I could not understand what they said. Bishop hailed me from the Churchyard and from within came the strains of the organ. He said Sir George Cornewall, the Rector was playing, but we need not be afraid of interrupting him. When Sir George had finished playing he came up into the Chancel and courteously showed me round the beautiful little Norman Church with its apse and stone altar.*

With its semi-circular apse Moccas Church is reminiscent of the one at Kilpeck and its walls are of a porous, spongy-textured material. This is a local stone called calcareous tufta, a stone formed by the deposit of water onto vegetable matter. There is 14th century stained glass in the windows showing the arms of the Fresne family on a red, white and blue standard carried by two yellow-clad figures. Their shield, with two brilliant green birds is in another window.

An effigy in the chancel is believed to represent Sir Reginald de Fresne who died in about 1330. When the Rev Rhys Bishop, Curate of Moccas, was showing Kilvert around Moccas Church, he drew his attention to this tomb. The Clyro curate was prompted to imagine that he was himself related to Sir Reginald on his mother's side, for the name Fresne, latinised to Fraximus (Ash) was equivalent to that of his maternal grandmother (named Ashe). By New Year's Day, 1878 this vague possibility had grown into fact in Kilvert's mind:

> *I told (James Davies) that the knight in armour whose recumbent figure rests upon the tomb in the chancel in Moccas Church was an ancestor of mine, and that my forefathers owned the Moccas estate. The Churchwarden opened his grey eyes incredulously...*

Effigy of Sir Reginald de Fresne who died in about 1330

Also of interest in the church is the tympanum above the Norman doorway which depicts two men clinging to the trunk of a tree as they are attacked by animals. A similar tympanum in the blocked north doorway is badly worn but used to show a carving of the Beast eating the Tree of Life.

**Moccas Court** has been the seat of the Cornewalls since 1771 after Sir George Aymund inherited a considerable fortune which enabled him to marry the heiress of an important Herefordshire family, Catherine Cornewall. But the condition was that he changed his name to hers and he duly complied. His grandson was the Rev Sir George Cornewall who is mentioned by Kilvert. He was rector of Moccas from 1861 until his death in 1908.

Moccas Court has been the seat of the Cornewalls for more than two centuries and the building is a Classical red-brick house built by a local man to the designs of Robert Adam, between 1775 and 1781. It has a beautiful circular drawing room decorated with French paper panels. The grounds were laid out by Capability Brown and Humphrey Repton in 1778.

Sir George Cornewall

Return up the drive and then join the main road (B4352), turning right by the war memorial. Shortly on the left you will pass **Moccas Deer Park** which is now a National Nature Reserve managed by English Nature. This medieval wooded 300 acre park contains a specimen of weeping oak, the largest tree of this variety known in England.

> *I walked up to the top of Moccas park, whence we had a glorious view of the Golden Valley shining in the evening sunlight with the white houses of Dorstone scattered about the green hillsides 'like a handful of pearls in a cup of emerald' and the noble spire of Peterchurch rising from out of the heart of the beautiful rich valley which was closed below by the Sugar Loaf and the Skyrrid blue above Abergavenny. We came tumbling and plunging down the steep hillside of Moccas Park, slipping, tearing and sliding through oak and birch and fallow wood of which there seemed to be underfoot an accumulation of several feet, the gathering ruin and decay probably of centuries. As we came down the lower slopes of the wooded hillside into the glades of the park the herds of deer were moving under the brown oaks and the brilliant green hawthorns, and we came upon the tallest stateliest ash I ever saw and what seemed at first in the dusk to be a great ruined tower, but which proved to be the vast ruin of the king oak of Moccas Park, hollow and broken but still alive and vigorous in parts and actually pushing out new shoots and branches. That tree may be 2000 years old. It measured roughly 33 feet round by arm stretching.*
>
> *I fear those grey old men of Moccas, those grey, gnarled low-browed, knock-kneed, bowed, bent, huge, strange, long-armed, deformed, hunchbacked misshapen oak men that stand waiting and watching century after century biding God's time with both feet in the grave and yet tiring down and seeing out generation after generation, with such tales to tell, as they whisper them to each other in the midsummer nights, make the silver birches weep and the poplars and aspens shiver and the long ears of the hares and rabbits stand on end. No human hand set those oaks. They are 'the trees which the Lord hath planted'. They look as if they had been at the beginning and making of the world, and they will probably see its end.*

Moccas Park has been established as the first ever parkland nature reserve and this is due to Richard Chester-Master (1927-1994) who inherited the Moccas Estate and was aware of its importance to naturalists.

One has to seek permission to enter this remarkable Nature Reserve, so otherwise just observe these remarkable oak trees whilst following the road to Bredwardine. Turn right opposite the red brick 17th century *Red Lion Inn* to pass another war memorial on the left. Then drive down a lane on the right which leads to **Bredwardine Church** (GR 334445) which will be seen directly ahead.

Bredwardine means 'the village on the bank' and is derived from *bred* meaning the brim or bank and *wardine* a homestead. It is beautifully situated in lush Herefordshire below Dorstone Hill and overlooking the Wye are the scanty remains of a castle founded by John de Bredwardine, who was granted the manor here at the time of the Conquest. Little is known of him and by 1227 the castle had become the property of the Baskerville family, one of whom Sir Walter Baskerville acquired it by marriage. When his son died without issue it passed for a time to a Cheshire family called Fouleshurst, but in 1493 it returned to the Baskervilles in the person of Sir John, great grand-son of Richard Baskerville, a brother of Sir Walter. Finally it passed to the Vaughans. By the fifteenth century it was in ruins and today only earthworks are remaining, all the stonework, except for a few remnants of the foundations, having been taken for the construction of local buildings.

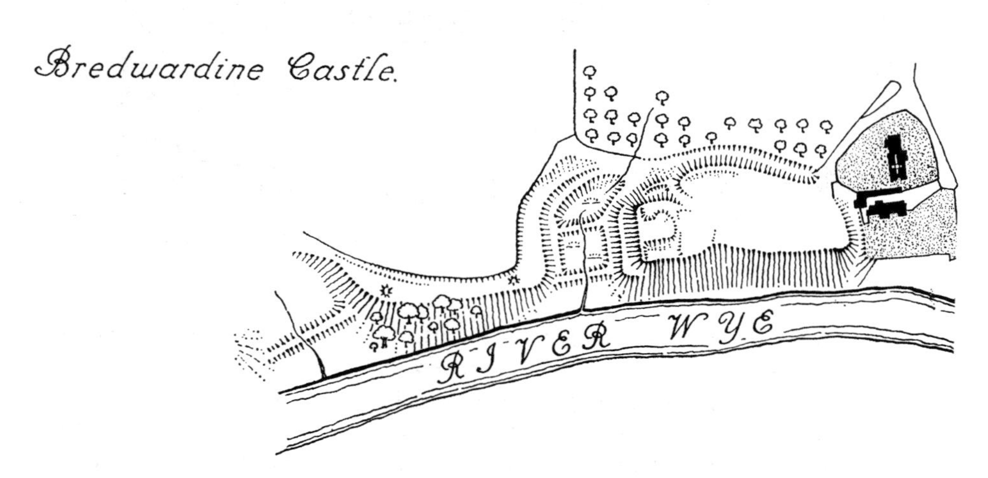


The earthworks of Bredwardine Castle stand on a little spur of land overhanging the river, to the south east of the churchyard. Of the masonry only a few traces of the foundations remain. A mansion was also built on this site by Sir Roger Vaughan in about 1640.

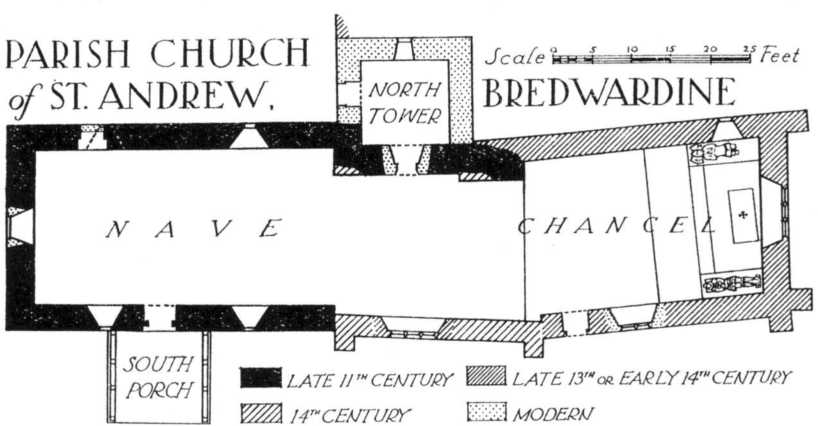


Bredwardine church was built soon after the Conquest and the nave still has its Norman windows and doorways. The chancel was added as an extension to the original eleventh century building in about 1300 and it is strangely askew. It is also unusual that the tower is on the north side of the church and it probably replaced an original central one when it was rebuilt in the 18th century. A Norman doorway on the north wall has been filled in but of interest is the elaborate lintel carved with a twisted column and a rosette on either side of two grotesque monsters, one like a monkey and the other resembling a pig on its hind legs.

Inside the church can be seen a fragment of a Norman coffin lid with a cross carved on it. The rather fine communion table at the west end was brought here from the old church at Brobury.

In the sanctuary are two remarkable effigies resting on tombs. One is a much battered 14th century figure of a knight in chain armour, with angels at his cushioned head. It represents Walter of Bredwardine who was the grandfather of the other effigy, a 15th century warrior in alabaster depicting Sir Roger Vaughan. He is clad from head to foot in plate armour and his head rests on his helmet. He is wearing the SS collar, a badge of the Lancastrians, said to stand for the first and last letters of the SENESCHALLUS, the title of John of Gaunt as Steward of England. Sir Roger was son-in-law to Sir Davy Gam and both these men fell at Agincourt while defending Henry V. Gam was knighted by the grateful king as he lay dying on the battlefield. Gwladys, the widow of Sir Roger Vaughan later married Sir William Herbert of Raglan Castle and is buried in St Mary's Priory Church at Abergavenny.

The large and roughly fashioned font, supported on four legs and a central shaft

14th century effigy of Walter of Bredwardine

15th century effigy in alabaster of Sir Roger Vaughan

Kilvert was offered the living at Bredwardine in September 1877 when the Vicar, Rev J. Houseman, died of a heart attack. Now 37 years of age, Kilvert must have felt that at last he had reached his goal, having waited so long for a living that really suited him. He was instituted to the living of Bredwardine on St Andrew's Day, 30th November 1877.

The vicarage, situated just behind the church is a very attractive building with a series of little round gables and large French windows providing pleasant views to the river. Kilvert's new home was furnished with items purchased from Schoolbreds in Tottenham Court Road, London. There were also pieces of furniture obtained from Bath.

Built in 1805 on the site of an older dwelling it was much larger in Kilvert's day, for after his death the servants' quarters were demolished. He had four servants and his sister Dora kept house for him before her marriage. Mrs Price was then appointed as housekeeper.

It was within these walls that Kilvert sat down at his desk to write the final pages of his *Diary*. The first entry here being on 31 December 1878, when he wrote: *A fine spring morning, bright sunshine, the river full, swift and brown, but falling; the cedars and the bright green lawn terraces very lovely in the morning sunshine.*

When his parents came to visit him at his new home in January 1878, Kilvert no doubt with considerable pride showed his father around the garden and the church:-

> *Showed my father round the garden and over the Church. He was much pleased with everything. The house and garden were much larger and more beautiful than he had supposed. Both he and my mother are delighted with the place. My father especially admired the old Norman 12th or 13th century work in the Church and more particularly the South doorway arch and the carving over the Devil's Door (the North door)*

It was indeed a good life at Bredwardine and an entry in the Diary for 24th February, 1878, shows how much Kilvert appreciated his new home and was very contented:

> *After luncheon I sat in the warm sheltered nook by the greenhouse looking down the river watching the lights changing, broadening, narrowing, vanishing on the soft dark stream. The sky was grey and silvery, very soft, pleasant and delicate, and the sun shone out warm by whiles. The willows were reddening with buds by the water courses. From the*

*lower garden came the rushing of a little brook or spring running into the river. Now and then a heavy fish jumped with a loud splash in the deep water off the garden, the birds were singing softly, the cooing of the woodpigeons came gently from the cedars and the river orchard, and the plaintive cry of the moorhens rose from the waterside. Then at 2 o' clock the 4 sweet bells rung an hour before service and from the Church came faint and sweet the roll of the organ.*

Bredwardine Vicarage became the home of Francis Kilvert in November 1877

He was in fact responsible now for two churches, for he also looked after **Brobury Church** on the other side of the Wye. Dedicated to St Mary Magdalene, it had been served by Bredwardine's priest from 1751 and the small parish united with Bredwardine in 1853. It was a small aisless structure comprising of just the chancel of the original medieval church, the nave having been demolished in 1873. It dated back to Norman times and still contained a font of that period. In *Domesday* the name of this place is Brochberie from broc 'stream ' and bury 'fort' - thus fort by the stream. This relates to the red sandstone cliff about half-a-mile to the east, called Brobury Scar, which has the remains of a prehistoric fort on its top.

> *My father wished much to go to Brobury in the evening but it rained and we thought it better for him to stay at home. There was an excellent congregation, the largest I have yet seen at Brobury Church. I preached from Matthew ii. 11, on the adoration of the Wise Men.*

In subsequent years Brobury Church fell into a ruined state and was sold in 1970 for conversion into a house. While the structure of the chancel has been saved, this private house has a rather strange modern tower at one end.

The living at Bredwardine was worth £350 a year to Kilvert which was more than three times the amount that he had been earning as a curate at Clyro. So he was now in a position to marry and that was indeed his intention. He had met his future wife, Elizabeth Rowland in Paris in 1876 on a visit arranged by his friend Mayhew. Elizabeth was the daughter of a landowner, John Rowland who lived in a fine house just outside Wootton near Woodstock in Oxfordshire.

Two of Elizabeth's nieces who wrote to the Kilvert Society in the 1940's described her as follows:

'She was tall, and her face had a very kind genial expression. She was unselfish, and ready to help anyone in trouble. The villagers of Wooton loved her. She had a Bible class of big girls on Sundays and was constantly visiting the sick and poor of the parish. She was fond of gardening and knew much about flowers. The birds in winter - even the rooks - came on the terrace when she fed them. Dogs knew, instinctively, that she would take them walks! Her manner was gentle and her voice soft: an excellent thing in a woman.'

Elizabeth Anne Kilvert appears in her photograph as a plain, rather prim, dowdily dressed lady, somewhat formidable in appearance and hardly the person that one might have expected Kilvert to marry for he always seemed to prefer more attractive ladies. The great love of his life had been 'Daisy' Thomas, whom he would have surely married, had not his beggarly curate's stipend been an insuperable barrier. We know little about Elizabeth apart from the fact that she came from Oxfordshire. After her husband's death she destroyed the notebooks containing details of their meeting, courtship and brief marriage.

# WALK 10

## *A Short Walk to Bredwardine Bridge and Brobury Gardens*

¼ mile (0.4 km)

When you have finished looking inside the church, turn right outside the churchyard gate and walk past the end of the old vicarage to go over a stile on the left. Then follow the path down through the fields to reach an iron gate opposite Bridge Cottage (old Toll House) and then on to Bredwardine Bridge. From the centre of this elegant structure is a good view of the vicarage and one can feel quite envious of Kilvert living in such a beautiful location.

The elegant brick bridge at Bredwardine

The bridge itself is also very fine and unusual, being built of brick with six arches. Erected in 1759 it joined the parishes of Bredwardine and Brobury and spanned a particularly beautiful stretch of the Wye, connecting the two main roads from Hereford to Hay-on-Wye. It is said to be the oldest brick bridge still in use in England. Kilvert mentions a flood in November, 1878, in which the Hereford coach was wrecked near the bridge because the coachman would not take the bearing reins off the horses and their heads were held under water.

*So far the greatest flood of this century. Before breakfast I went down to the bridge to see how the Jenkins family were. Soon after I passed last night the river came down with a sudden rush and wave and filled the road full of water and they had to escape to the trap, carrying their children on their backs, wading through water knee deep, and leaving 3 feet of water in the house, the house also being surrounded by water and the water running in at front and back. Mr Stokes kindly rode down from the Old Court to see if they were safe, the water was then up to his horse's girths. Many people were flooded out of their houses at Letton and Staunton and spent the night on Bredwardine Bridge watching the flood. A number of cattle and colts were seen to pass under the bridge in the moonlight and it was feared they would be drowned. Some women saw a bullock swept down under the bridge at noon to-day. Mr W. Clarke told me that the Whitney iron railway bridge was carried away last night by the flood and 2 miles of line seriously damaged. No trains can run for 3 months, during which time the gap will be filled by coaches.*

You may like to go over the bridge and up the road a short way to Brobury Gardens which are open to the public at certain times of the year. The house was built in the 1880s in the style of a Scottish hunting lodge. The formal Victorian gardens are particularly fine, providing magnificent views and there is also an art gallery specialising in British prints, maps and watercolours.

# WALK 11

## *Above Bredwardine*

3 ¼ miles (5.2km)

Follow the bridleway track to the right of Bredwardine church, passing the annexe graveyard on the right, in which Kilvert's wife is buried. Go through a small hunting gate and follow the sunken path around to the right. It passes below the mound on which Bredwardine Castle may have once stood. This is a confusing site for a mansion was also built on it by Roger Vaughan in about 1640. It later passed to the Cornewall family who dismantled the building and took the stone to Moccas Court in 1775-81.

An alternative site for a castle at Bredwardine was discovered in 1970 at the south end of the village (GR 337440). Here was revealed the base of a small stone tower and coins of Edward I or II, dating from 1275-1377.

On reaching a division in the path, keep to the right, walking on through the trees. Go through a gate, with glimpses of the Wye. In due course, below on the left will be seen a large fishpond. The path leads on with a wooden board walk spanning a wet area. Ignore the stile immediately on the right and continue, shortly passing a now redundant stile. The path then curves around to the right to reach a stile beside a gate.

Fork immediately left to follow the path to the left along the edge of a field, over a rise and on beside a fence. Go through a gap in a corner of the field and on between a fence and trees through which the Wye is occasionally glimpsed.

Go over a stile beside a gate and from here, directly opposite, on the other side of the river, can be seen the former Brobury Church, now a residenc with a strange modern tower. Further down the valley will be seen the red sandstone cliff known as Brobury Scar.

Continue down the field keeping the fence on your right to reach a stile. Then follow a track beside a hedge to reach the B4352. Turn right and follow the road with care. Moccas Park is now seen on the left with its ancient oak trees (see page 218 for description). In due course you will reach a lane on the left bearing the sign 'Bodcott Farm' (shown on OS Map as 'Lower Bodcott Farm').

Opposite the farmhouse go through a gate by a fingerpost and head straight across a field with open views to the right over this beautiful part of Herefordshire. The path meets a fence and then crosses a small stream to reach a stile in the corner of the field. Then go left beside a fence to reach another stile. Look to the right now to see Bredwardine Church.

## Walk 11 - Above Bredwardine

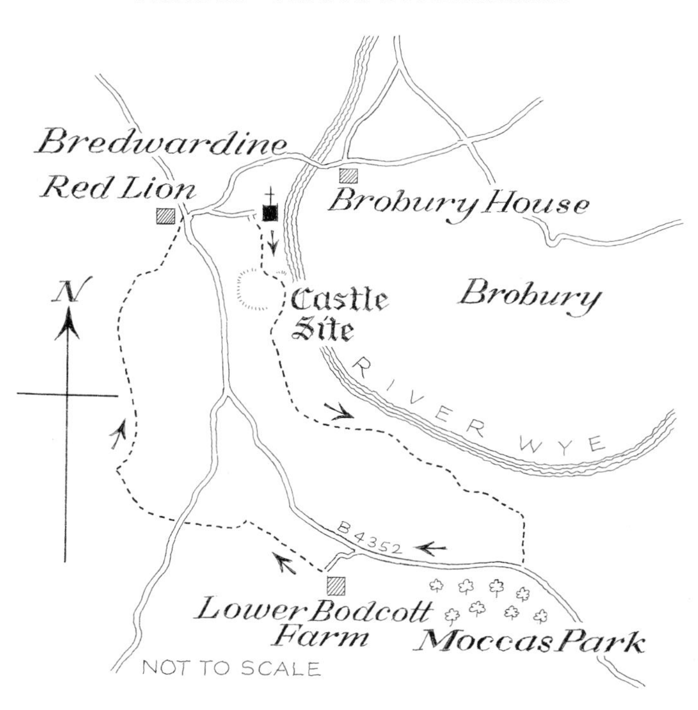

The *Red Lion Hotel* in Bredwardine

Head diagonally right across the next field to reach a stile on the top of a bank. Then bear slightly left across the next field to a stile beside a gate. On a clear day Clee Hill in Shropshire can be seen from here.

Cross the Dorstone Road and follow a tarmac drive for a few yards and then a hedge lined lane, passing above a fine stone built house ('Prospect'), which enjoys a fine view. Further on, pass in front of 'Old House Farm' and continue through two gates in quick succession. Then head diagonally down the field on your right (towards Bredwardine Church), to find a stile in the hedge.

Go straight across the next field to reach another stile beside a gate. Ignore the bridlepath gate on the right and continue along a path curving above a hollow to reach a stile beside a gate. Continue with a hedge on your right to reach a stile by a holly tree in the corner of the field. Now bear right, descending a rutted path to reach a stile in the hedge directly ahead. Ignore the waymarked path to the left and right and go straight across the field to reach a stile to the left of a timbered building. Immediately, cross a stile on the right to pass behind the building and and follow a lane down to the *Red Lion Hotel* in Bredwardine. Cross the road, to pass a war memorial and shortly go right along the lane leading to your starting point at Bredwardine Church.

The large porch of Bredwardine Church

## A PREMATURE ENDING

Kilvert's health now began to deteriorate and possibly this was partly due to a long period of rain and damp misty conditions. He talks of *a thick dark mild morning with a Scotch mist* and by mid-February he is spending *a day indoors nursing a bad cold and a troublesome cough.*

On Sunday 3rd March he walks in the churchyard: *in the fresh sweet sunny air, full of the singing of the birds and the brightness and gladness of spring.* Yet at the same time he expresses melancholy thoughts:

> *The southern side of the churchyard was crowded with a multitude of tombstones. They stood thick together, some taller, some shorter, some looking over the shoulders of others, and as they stood up all looking one way and facing the morning sun they looked like a crowd of men, and it seemed as if the morning of the Resurrection had come and the sleepers had arisen from their graves and were standing upon their feet, silent and solemn, all looking toward the East to meet the Rising of the Sun.*

Two days later Kilvert, in need of maternal care, went to stay with his parents at Langley Burrell and he records how the doctor told him that he had congestion of the lungs: *This evening I was worse than I have been at all, and could hardly draw breath from the tightness of the chest.*

A few days later he had recovered enough to take a walk on the terrace and wrote in his diary:

> *I went out for a little while on the terrace this morning and walked up and down on the sunny side of the house. After how many illnesses such as this have I taken my first convalescent walk on the sunny terrace and always at this time of the year when the honeysuckle leaves were shooting green and the apricot blossoms were dawning and the daffodils in blow. But some day will come the last illness from which there will be no convalescence...*

By the end of March he had returned to Bredwardine but he was still a sick man: *Indoors all day with a bad headache and fresh cold and great tightness of chest.* His cough became worse and *Lady Cornewall (of Moccas Court) called and kindly brought me another bottle of the syrup of Hypophosphate of Lime.*

At a vicarage garden party in Eardisley, Kilvert was offered the chance of a permanent chaplaincy at Cannes in the South of France by Canon Walsham. He gave careful consideration to the suggestion but decided to remain in Bredwardine.

His health improved a little during the fine summer of 1878, but in the autumn the weather deteriorated. The Wye was in flood and he recorded that *it was the second great flood of this century*.

By early December he was ill again and wrote: *Indoors all day with a bad sore throat, very hoarse, stupefied and stunned*.

That bad weather continued through December: *Fine and cold in the morning, overcast in the afternoon, glass falling and snow threatening*. A few days before Christmas he went for a walk and took obvious enjoyment in the wintry scenes:

> *As I went up the steep snowy hill to Bethell I pursued the fast retreating and ascending warm sunshine of the still winter afternoon. I overtook the sunshine just before I got to the lone house on the bleak wintry hilltop. All the valley and plain lay bathed in a frosty rosy glow, and just as I got to Cae Perthay the sun was setting behind the lone level snowy blue-white line of the Black Mountain and the last rays were reddening the walls and chimney stack of the solitary cottage.*

The River Wye froze over and Kilvert still continued to visit his beloved parishioners despite the very cold weather. He records how he *climbed up the steep icy bank to Godsalls, with great difficulty*.

The hard frost made the roads difficult to negotiate:

> *Hard Frost. I reached the school with great difficulty owing to the icy state of the roads especially on the hillside. Called at the Cottage. Miss Newton has given a text to Bredwardine Church for Christmas and an I.H.S. banner to Brobury. Advent service in Bredwardine Church at 7 p.m. Sir George Cornewall walked over from Moccas to preach, coming through the field and supporting himself with a spud walking stick. Between 30 and 40 people in Church which we thought a fair congregation considering the weather and icy roads.*

*Very hard frost. The Wye froze across below Bredwardine Bridge between the Vicarage garden and Brobury Shore. It has been frozen over and the ice passable for some time at Moccas. Visited Priscilla Price and took her a pudding and some mince pies for Christmas. Snow deep on the hill.*

*Very hard frost last night* (Christmas Day 1878). *At Presteign the thermometer fell to 2 degrees, showing 30 degrees of frost. At Monnington it fell to 4. Last night is said to have been the coldest night for 100 years. The windows of the house and Church were so thick with frost rime that we could not see out. We could not look through the Church windows all day. Snow lay on the ground and the day was dark and gloomy with a murky sky. A fair morning congregation considering the weather..*

*Sudden thaw and break up of the frozen river. Huge masses and floes of ice have been coming down the river all day rearing, crushing, grinding against each other, and thundering against the bridge. A crowd of people were on the bridge looking over the parapet and watching the ice pass through the arches. The ground very slippery and dangerous, people walking along the ditches and going on all fours up Bredwardine Hill and across the Lion Square. Emma Jones' mother came all the way from Dorstone to Bredwardine in the ditches. Price was obliged to go up the hill from the Cottage to his house on all fours and Jane Davies of Fine Street confessed to Dora that she had to crawl on the ice across the Lion Square on her hands and knees.*

*It was very slippery and dangerous as I went to Brobury. Coming back the water was out across the lane and giving Clara Powell my lantern to hold I carried her in my arms across the water.*

(Sunday, 29th December, 1878)

The last day in December (1878) brought fine weather and Kilvert tells us how he paid a visit to Mr and Mrs Jenkins who kept the bridge toll gate at Bredwardine:-

> *A fine mild spring morning, bright sunshine, the river full, swift and brown, but falling, the cedars and the bright green lawn terraces very lovely in the morning sunshine. As I crossed Bredwardine Bridge I went to see the Jenkinses who have kept the bridge toll gate for 2 months. They seem nice old people. The old woman was full of strange stories of the countryside. She had felt beforehand and predicted the coming of the great rainstorm and waterspout which fell on the Eppynt Hills in the summer of 1854 in July, and swept away the Lawrence's house on the Dihonn brook near Builth. She had lived for years at the Holly Bush on the northern slope of the Black Mountain and her husband had kept school in the Baptist Chapel at Capel y Ffin. 'There are strange things about the Black Mountain,' she said, 'but I have travelled the hills at all hours, night and day, and never saw anything bad. One time I had been working late at the Parc on the southern side of the Mountain down in the dingle and I was coming home pretty late in the dark. It was about February or March. As I came over the Bwlch y fingel I was singing to keep my courage up, and I was singing a hymn out of an old book for I thought I wouldn't sing anything but was good then. It was a fine starlight night and just as I got down into the plain I heard beautiful singing overhead, like the singing of birds. They seemed to be some great birds travelling. I could not see them but they sang and whistled most beautiful, and they were just overhead. They seemed to be going away down the mountain towards Caedwgan. And I said to myself, 'God bless me from here, there will be a funeral from that house', and sure enough within a month a dead person was carried out from Caedwgan.*
>
> (Monday 31st December, 1878)

On New Year's Day, 1879, Kilvert recorded how he had sat up the previous night to see the old year out and the new year in. Little did he know that he would never have the chance to do this again:-

> *I was up last night to watch the old year out and the new year in. The Church bells rang at intervals last night and all to-day. At 6 I went to Crafta Webb to begin my cottage lectures there.*

*It was raining fast when I started, but when I got as far as the Common I noticed that the ground was white. At first I thought it was moonlight. Then I saw it was snow. At Crafta Webb the snowstorm was blinding and stifling, and I passed by Preece's cottage where I was going to hold the lecture without seeing it in the thickness of the driving snow. Before the lecture I went in to see old John Williams. On opening the door I was confronted by the motionless silent figure of a person veiled and wearing a comical cap which I presently discovered to be a dead pig hanging up by its snout. John Williams deplored my being out in such a night and said it was not fit for me. There were not many people at the service but the usual faithful few. When I came back the storm was worse and so thick and driving that I was glad I was between hedges and not out on the open hill.*

Crafta Webb was a group of cottages on the hill behind the *Red Lion* and in one of these small dwellings Kilvert gave his 'cottage lectures'. The community has now virtually disappeared.

By February the weather had improved and Kilvert records: *The birds are beginning to sing again by the river after the hard frost and the long winter.*
At the end of February, 1879, he observed how the recent freeze had caused damage to walls at the vicarage garden and Brobury churchyard:-

> *Walking in the garden in the evening I discovered that the intense frost of last month had caused a slip and settlement of the rail on the terrace walk and caused the wall supporting the terrace to bulge dangerously. A large slice of the Vicarage river bank just below the hydraulic ram has slipped into the river, the churchyard wall has bulged, Brobury Churchyard wall has been thrown down by the frost, the walls all over the place have been strained and shaken, the plaster is peeling and shelling off the house and conservatory, and the steps from the upper to the lower garden are in ruins. This is the work of the frost of 1878-1879.*

On 12th March 1879, Kilvert wrote: *When I came home from Moccas last night, Dora showed me a letter received today from James Pitcairn asking her to marry him. This took me entirely by surprise, but I forsee that she will do so.* In due course Kilvert had to employ a housekeeper. But what he really need was a wife and he had met his chosen spouse, Elizabeth Rowland during a holiday in Paris three years earlier. Unfortunately all details of their courtship were removed from the *Diary* by Kilvert's widow after his death.

The *Diary* ceases on Thursday 13th March, 1879, a few months before Kilvert's death. There may of course be a subsequent notebook entries which have not been discovered or were destroyed by his widow. In his last entry he is still describing visits to local people, admiring the scenery of the Wye Valley as he goes. He speaks of a lovely cloudless day and describes views of the Black Mountains with snow patches. He walks home to Bredwardine from Kinnersley and concludes, *A sharp frost and the north-west wind bitterly cold.*

On the 20th of August 1879, Francis Kilvert married Elizabeth Anne Rowland at Wootton-by-Woodstock which is not far from Blenheim Palace. They had known each other for three years, having met during Kilvert's tour of Paris (1876) which he mentions in the *Diary*. Elizabeth Rowland was the daughter of John Rowland of Hollybank, Wootton and one of seven children. Her father had begun medical studies at St Thomas and Guy's Hospitals, London, but instead became a landowner after inheriting property in Oxfordshire.

The honeymoon was spent in Scotland and they returned to Bredwardine on the 13th of September to a wonderful, warm welcome by the village people, as described in the following report which appeared in the *Hereford Times* on October 4th 1879:

> The inhabitants of Bredwardine and Brobury on Saturday last welcomed to their home their Vicar and his wife. Though rain fell all day, and drenched those who were not encased in material waterproof, it did not seem to quench the warmth with which the poorer people of Bredwardine brought flowers, made nosegays, decorated poles, and hung upon them inscriptions of 'WELCOME HOME'. This was the work which they were all either engaged in, or looking at, criticising or approving. And all this work of hearty love was being carried out because they had been informed that they might expect their pastor - The Rev R.F. Kilvert, home that evening after his marriage which, we are informed, took place on 20th August, at Wooton, Woodstock; a place of some historical interest, as being the place where Fair Rosamund is said to have been poisoned by Queen Eleanor.
>
> The first archway was erected at 'Church Turn', the entrance of the drive from the high road to the church, and was a mass of flowers and evergreens - very well disposed, with a motto, 'Welcome Home', the painting being the work of a local genius, and the decoration that of Miss Annie Lewis of Clappits Cottage. The second was at the entrance to the Vicarage, and was erected under the instruction of the Misses Newton, of The Cottage. The words 'Welcome Home' were enclosed on either side with the initials of the happy pair, all being well wrought in ornamental letters, and the whole structure decorated with bannerets. Over the entrance to the Vicarage were various artistic designs and mottos, the whole being made to look as attractive and festive as possible. But conspicuous amongst the many and various demonstrations of hearty welcome in the parish of Brobury were two triumphal arches of elegant design, bearing appropriate mottos for the occasion. The first stood opposite the residence of Mr Williams of Brobury Court and bespoke much taste, pains and care; the second near the residence of Mr James Powell, coal agent etc, which was quite a model of good taste, the construction being solely due to the exertions and industry of Miss J. Powell.
>
> Under the giant limbs of a very fine cedar, extended over the gravelled entrance to the Vicarage, tables covered with snow-white cloths, were spread for a tea, with which the school children were first regaled, then the old women, and lastly sober-minded men, such as chose to partake of it. The tables were tended by the Rev W.R. and Mrs Smith of Monnington; the Rev Rhys Bishop of Moccas; the Rev

and Mrs A. Pope of Blakemere; Miss Palmer of Eardisley; Miss Stokes of the Old Court; the Misses Davies, The Weston; Miss A. Davies; Miss Sarah and Miss Eliza Abberley; Mr and Miss Bates; Mr Algernon Bates; Miss Wilmot; Mrs Price; Miss Jones, Crafta Webb; Mrs B. Hammond and Miss F. Smith. Everything was done to make their guests happy. The Misses Newton came down in their carriage and remained during the evening.

A committee of farmers (with Mr Stokes of the Old Court as secretary) had collected certain moneys, with which they had purchased half a dozen silver dessert forks and half a dozen dessert spoons with a caddy spoon. These gentlemen were Mr F. Evans, The Weston; Mr Davies, Fine Street; Mr Jones, Cross-End; Mr Griffiths, The Pentre; and Mr Jenkins.

Mr George Price, the coachman to the Misses Newton of The Cottage, had set to work among the cottagers, and soon got enough money to purchase a very handsome and massive pair of solid silver gravy spoons.

About five o' clock a band of labourers crossed the picturesque old bridge at Bredwardine and went towards Brobury, where they shortly met the carriage containing the happy pair, who were received with the waving of banners and hearty shouts. After re-crossing the river to the Bredwardine side, the horses were taken from the carriage, ropes attached thereto, and amidst hearty cheering the happy pair were safley drawn to the Vicarage door.

Mr Frank Evans, of The Weston, the churchwarden, came forward (with the presentation from the tenant farmers and others) and read the following address, which had been printed in gold, within a floriated border:- TO THE REV R. F. KILVERT MA, VICAR OF BREDWARDINE, ON HIS MARRIAGE. Reverend Sir - It is with heartfelt pleasure and gratitude that we, tenant farmers, occupiers, and others of the Parish of Bredwardine, assemble on this occasion to offer you our sincere congratulations on the auspicious event of your marriage. As the pastor of this important parish, we have had ample means for judging your personal worth and Christian character, and rejoice to have this opportunity of testifying to our appreciation of and admiration of the same by asking you to accept from us a small token of our esteem, which we are sure you will value, not for its intrinsic value, which is small, but as an outcome of generous wishes on our part for your future happiness and that of your amiable partner, throughout life. In making to you and Mrs Kilvert this small presentation of domestic articles - the use of which will no doubt frequently recall to you this important and pleasurable epoch along the road of life - allow us to express a hope that God will bless you and yours with a prolonged and useful existence, health and happiness, and crown your Christian labours with their well deserved reward. September 13th 1879.

*The Rev Gentleman said* :- Mr Evans, dear friends and neighbours; believe me this most kind reception given to me and my dear wife on our return home has taken me by the greatest surprise, for I really did not expect anything of the kind. Much less did I expect such a mark of respect from the dear little children, who have so kindly flocked around us; and which I assure you I feel most deeply. Dear friends and neighbours, you have not only congratulated me on my return home, but also my dear wife, who is a stranger to you, but who feels the compliment as deeply as I do, and who, although you do not know her yet, you will in time learn to love as much as you have today shown you do me. Believe me, words fail to express half the gratification I feel at receiving this very handsome present at your hands. Mr Evans has spoken of the testimonial as but a slight mark of your esteem, but I assure you I think its intrinsic value very considerable, and I do value these articles most highly as a token of your regard for me. I do hope that I have the real affection of my parishioners, and that the kind way in which you have come forward today to welcome me and my dear wife will draw us nearer together in heart and mind than ever (cheers). It has ever been, believe me, the aspiration of my heart that we may live in confidence, and love one another as members of one great Christian family, and I sincerely trust (as I said before) that this kind of reception will draw us nearer together and cement our hearts in Christian unity. (Applause). Although the rain has made the weather most unfavourable for out-of-door enjoyments, I hope you will regard this as a bright and happy day, when you welcomed your clergyman after his marriage (applause). Once more accept my thanks for your great kindness today and ever since I have been here, and I assure you I have learned to love you more and more since I came here. I wish I could entertain you all better than I am able to on this occasion, but I hope you will be as comfortable as possible under the circumstances. I thank you again for your beautiful presents, which I shall value as some of the greatest treasures I possess. (Applause).

Mr Bates then stepped forward (with a pair of heavy silver tablespoons in a morocco case), and read the following address from the cottagers, also printed in gold and bordered:-

To the Rev R.F. Kilvert, MA, Vicar of Bredwardine on his marriage. Rev Sir, - We your Parishioners, being Cottagers and others of Bredwardine are delighted to have this occasion of acknowledging the kind and Christian interest you have since your residence in this parish, ever manifested for our social and spiritual welfare, and pray God that your recent union to the amiable lady of your choice may increase your happiness an hundredfold. As a slight token of the esteem and respect which we have always held you and which we

> sincerely hope may never be interrupted, but year by year be strengthened and matured - we beg of you and Mrs Kilvert to accept this small presentation of silver from us, both as a memento of the love we bear you and yours, and of the auspicious event which has brought us together.
> September 13th, 1879.
>
> *After a pause, the Rev Gentleman replied* :- My dear friends, I am more than deeply touched and moved by your kind reception, love and affection towards me. Much as I am taken by surprise by the last beautiful gift from my friends who occupy good positions in life, this touches me more deeply still, because I know it is given from slender incomes and pockets not very deep. This beautiful gift has, I believe, been prompted by a love which I feel I very little deserve (No, No). But if God spares me I will try to deserve your affection and show you how deeply grateful I am for these kind efforts today (applause). I hope, not withstanding that the rain - coming down as it does - has made it unpleasant, that you have still sunshine in your hearts, and that you will try to make yourselves as happy as you possibly can. To you I also say that I am sorry that I cannot entertain so large a company any better than I have done, but hope you will be content with what I can do. I hope that you may all live long, and that the longer we live the more closely we may be drawn together in the bonds of Christian love. God bless you all, I can say no more. (Applause).

These are the final words of Kilvert that have been recorded. Unfortunately, although he seemed to be in high spirits and good health, he started complaining of not feeling well the day after his return to Bredwardine. In fact it was necessary for his father, who was staying at Kilvert's home at the time, to take the morning service, while Andrew Pope (now Vicar of Blakemere), took the evening service at Brobury.

Kilvert's condition rapidly deteriorated and it would seem that he was suffering with an appendicitis which turned to peritonitis, for which at that time there was no known cure. He died on Tuesday 23rd September, just five weeks after his wedding and a fortnight after his return from his honeymoon.

Kilvert's death and funeral was reported in the *Hereford Times* on 4th October 1879:

> A more lamentable occurrence it has not fallen to our lot for some time to chronicle the death of Rev R.F. Kilvert, which took place on Tuesday, the 23rd of September, after a very short illness, and not five weeks after his wedding day. It was only on the 20th September that the *Hereford Times* contained an interesting report of the return home

of Mr Kilvert and of the joyous welcome given to, and the numerous presents received by them, the inhabitants from the highest to the lowest all striving to show their affection and esteem. The news of his illness and decease coming so quickly afterwards struck with surprise and sharp sorrow many residents not only in the neighbourhood of Bredwardine, where he was so beloved, but throughout the county.

The funeral, a simple unostentatious one, in accordance with the wishes of the deceased, took place on Saturday last. The weather was exceedingly gloomy and depressing, enough to intensify the melancholy that filled the hearts of the mourners, for hardly a breath of air stirred, and the sun strove unsuccessfully to break through the sombre, misty clouds, which from showers occasionally descended, the sunlight appearing to be reflected glaringly above the clouds, and the lovely wooded scenery of the Wye looked wet and dull. As the vicarage is only about sixty yards from Bredwardine church, the sad proceedings did not occupy a very long time. Eight bearers, parishioners, carried the coffin which was covered with a dark velvet pall and the mourners who followed were:- Mrs R.F. Kilvert, and her father Mr. J. Rowland; the deceased's four sisters - Mrs W. R. Smith, Monnington; Mrs Wyndowe, London; Miss F. Kilvert and Mrs Pitcairn, London (who had formerly resided at Bredwardine Vicarage); Rev R. Kilvert, Rector of Langley Burrell, Wiltshire (father of deceased), Mr E. N. Kilvert (brother); and the Rev W. R. Smith of Monnington. The funeral party also included Mr F. Evans, Weston; and Mr T. Stokes, Old Court (church wardens); Mr Bates, Bredwardine; and other farmers; six Foresters, members of Moccas 'Court' (of which deceased was an honourary member) wearing their scarves; and a large number of cottagers and schoolchildren. The cortege slowly passed under the giant limbs of a fine old cedar tree, near where a fortnight before the Vicar had watched with pleasure the children and the old people regaled with tea, and it was met in the church gate by the deceased's venerable friend, the Rev R. L. Venables, who read very touchingly the first part of the Burial Service of the Church. In the sacred edifice the procession was met by the Rev Sir G. H. Cornewall, Bt, of Moccas (lord of the manor), the Rev Henry Dew, Rector of Whitney; Rev C. S. Palmer, Vicar of Eardisley; Rev F. Andrews, Rector of Kinnersley; etc. The psalms and the Lesson having been read - there was no singing - the cortege moved to the grave which is situated on the north side of the church, next to the road. Some beautiful wreaths were placed on the coffin by the mourners, and the school children afterwards put a number of wreaths and other floral emblems into the grave. The coffin was of oak, with white metal furniture, the inscription being - 'Robert Francis Kilvert, died Sept. 23rd 1879, aged 38', Mr A. C. Edwards, High Town, Hereford, was the undertaker.

The white tombstone of Rev Francis Kilvert, photographed on the anniversary of his death on 23rd September, 2000. He must have known that he was going to end his days at Bredwardine for he chose this spot for his own grave on 13th February, 1878, *close by the stile leading onto the castle garden, beside the path by which people came to church.* The quotation 'He, being dead, yet speaketh' is also on his father's tombstone at Langley Burrell churchyard in Wiltshire.

Buried in the graves either side of Kilvert are Miss Julia Louisa Newton and her sister Catherine. They lived in 'The Cottage' (now known as Bredwardine Hall) and were both very fond of Kilvert. But, having been buried either side of him, no space was left for Mrs Kilvert who as a result had to be laid to rest in the new churchyard on the other side of the road.

Mrs Kilvert, as a clergyman's widow was now homeless for she had to leave the vicarage and she returned to her father's home at Wootton, Oxfordshire. She survived her husband for just over 30 years and every year as long as she was able, she returned to Bredwardine to place flowers on his grave. In 1911 she died at Redlands, Hartfield Road, Eastbourne and her body was brought to Bredwardine for burial.

The grave of Elizabeth Kilvert is similar to that of her husband

After Kilvert's death a poem written by him was found in his blotter. The last verse seems to indicate that he knew that he did not have long to live:-

*Let him sing a little while in peace, his songs will soon be o'er,*
*And the singer spreads his wings with joy to find a happier shore,*
*When the nest is found forsaken, some will smile, and some will sigh,*
*For the voice which now no longer mingles with the murmuring Wye.*

*27th May, 1879, Eos Gwy*

It is interesting that this poem bears a date later than that on which the Diary ends and Kilvert only had four months to live when he penned these words

The Kilvert Society has erected a stone seat near the churchyard entrance, under a large yew tree. It is inscribed: *'To the memory of Francis Kilvert'*,

And so here at Bredwardine in the beautiful Wye Valley, we reach the end of our journey bringing to a close the story of the Reverend Francis Kilvert. Either return to Hay on the B4532 or carry on along the road over Bredwardine Bridge, to turn immediately left up the lane leading to the A438. Turn left and follow this road back to Clyro, the sleepy little village which will always be identified as the heart of *Kilvert Country*.

# GENERAL INFORMATION

## Tourist Information Centres

Information and details of bed & breakfast, hotels, bunkhouses, camping etc. available from:-

*Abergavenny*
Swan Meadow, Monmouth Road
Abergavenny NP7 5HH
Tel: 01873 857588
(Open all year)

*Builth Wells*
The Groe Car Park, Builth Wells,
Powys LD2 3BT
Tel: 01982 553307
(Seasonal)

*Hay-on-Wye*
Oxford Road, Hay-on-Wye HR3 5DG
Tel: 01497 820144
(Open all year)

*Hereford*
1, King Street, Hereford HR4 9BW
Tel: 01432 342662
(Open all year)

*Kington*
2, Mill Street, Kington HR5 3BQ
Tel: 01544 230778
(Seasonal)

*Rhyader*
The Leisure Centre, North Street,
Rhyader LD6 5BU
Tel: 01597 810591
(Open all year)

*Talgarth*
The Tower Shop, Talgarth LD3 0BW
Tel: 01874 712226
(Seasonal)

## Visitor Centres and Attractions

*The Kilvert Gallery*, Clyro
Contemporary art gallery in the former home of the Rev Francis Kilvert.
Tel: 01497 820033

*Brobury Gardens*, Bredwardine - 5 acres of formal Victorian Gardens and 2 acres of water meadows open to the public. Tel: 01981 500229

*Erwood Station* - A picturesque rural railway station beside the Wye. Refreshments, picnic site and craft shop.
Tel: 01982 560674
(Open mid-Feb to end of Dec)

## Suggested Web Sites

Churches:
www.churchinwales.org.uk/swanbrec/541

Hay-on-Wye:-
www.hay-on-wye.co.uk

Herefordshire: www.aph.org.uk
Talgarth:-
www.talgarthtic.demon.co.uk/

Kilvert Society:-
www.communigate.co.uk/here/kilvertsociety/index.phtml.

*The Kilvert Society was set up in 1948 to keep alive an interest in Francis Kilvert, his diaries and the countryside he loved. The Society meets several times a year for seminars and walks etc. A journal is also published three times a year.*

## FURTHER READING

*After Kilvert*, A.L. Le Quesne, (Oxford University Press), 1978
*Collected Verse by Francis Kilvert* (The Kilvert Society), 1975
*Cymru Kilvert*, Trebor Lloyd (A Welsh translation of part of the *Diary*), 1973
*Francis Kilvert: Priest and Diarist*, F. Grice (The Kilvert Society), 1975
*Francis Kilvert and his World*, Frederick Grice, (Caliban Books), 1983
*Kilvert's Bredwardine*, Kenneth R. Clew, 1970
*Kilvert's Diary* 1870 - 1879, edited by William Plomer, (Jonathan Cape), 1938-40
*Who's Who in Kilvert's Diary*, F. Grice, (The Kilvert Society), 1977
*Francis Kilvert*, David Lockwood (Seren Books), 1990
*Kilvert: The Homeless Heart*, John Toman (Logaston Press), 2000
*Kilvert's Clyro Now*, Eugene Fisk (A & K Publications), 2000

## OTHER TITLES BY CHRIS BARBER

*Walks in the Brecon Beacons*
*Exploring the Waterfall Country*
*Ghosts of Wales*
*Exploring the Brecon Beacons National Park*
*Exploring Gwent*
*Mysterious Wales*
*More Mysterious Wales*
*Cordell Country*
*The Romance of the Welsh Mountains*
*Hando's Gwent (Volume 1)*
*Hando's Gwent (Volume 2)*
*The Ancient Stones of Wales* (Jointly with J.G. Williams)
*The Seven Hills of Abergavenny*
*Journey to Avalon* (Jointly with David Pykitt)
*Arthurian Caerleon*
*Abergavenny in Old Picture Postcards*
*Portraits of the Past*
*Classic Walks in the Brecon Beacons National Park*
*In Search of Owain Glyndwr*
*Eastern Valley - The Story of Torfaen*
*Exploring Blaenavon Industrial Landscape World Heritage Site*